the years. He has learned what works and why. With Msgr. Francis Friedl, he now shares that rich background in *Homilies Alive*."

Bishop Edward J. O'Donnell
Administrator, Archdiocese of St. Louis

"This book on preaching is uniquely excellent and will be well received. While the authors support the fundamental requisites for effective proclaiming of the Good News, namely, the presence of a vibrant faith life in the preacher, and the skills needed to deliver a clear and focused message, they direct their attention here toward helping the homilist acquire the skills needed to achieve effective communication."

Rev. Paul C. Reinert, S.J.
St. Louis University

"*Homilies Alive* is not only a 'what to' and 'why to' book, but also a wise and practical 'how to' book on writing and delivering homilies that move the heart and mind. This well written, solid guide will be valuable for preachers, lectors, and liturgists, indeed, for anyone interested in communicating with skill and integrity. It is a superb reality check for those dedicated to the good use of the spoken and written word."

Louise Collins
Host/Producer, The Louise Collins Show

"This book is written with an exciting pastoral touch. For those with limited time to read, it is a perfect book, a great gift for pastors or pastoral associates. Its ideas are based on solid principles for excellence in oral communication today. The authors write clear and concise recommendations for effective preaching. This book should be required for seminary formation and clergy renewal programs."

Sr. Angela Ann Zukowski, MHSH, D. Min.
Director, Center for Religious Communication

"*Homilies Alive* is a clear, readable, and concise exploration of the process of creating a homily. It serves well as a text for beginning homiletic students and as a good review for veteran preachers."

Ed Ruane, O.P. and Regina Siegfried, A.S.C.
Editors, *In the Company of Preachers*

"*Homiles Alive* reflects the depth, enthusiasm, and spirituality of two able writers and observers. It deals with the problems and the possibilities of this central part of our ministry. I hope the book reaches the hands and hearts of thousands of preachers."

Msgr. John Sheridan
Author, Retired Pastor, Our Lady of Malibu Parish

Forewords by
JOE GARAGIOLA
DANIEL W. KUCERA, OSB
Archbishop of Dubuque

HOMILIES
Alive
CREATING HOMILIES THAT HIT HOME

Msgr. Francis P. Friedl
and Ed Macauley

TWENTY-THIRD PUBLICATIONS
Mystic, Connecticut

ACKNOWLEDGMENTS

We would like to acknowledge many people who have both encouraged and assisted in the work of publishing this book.

Special thanks from Monsignor Friedl go to Rex Reynolds, Professor of Speech and Communication at Loras College, Dubuque, who spent an incalculable number of hours reading the text, offering invaluable suggestions during the writing, and serving as mentor for the development of the structure of the book. Thanks is extended also to George and Lillian Freund for their proofreading; Professor Thomas Goodman of the Loras College faculty for the final two proofreadings and suggestions for emendations; and finally to Kevin White, who initiated the collaborative effort of Friedl and Macauley.

Deacon Macauley wishes to express grateful appreciation to his wife Jackie, who has encouraged him through the entire period of time he worked on this volume; and to Rev. Joseph Naumann and Rev. Denis Daly for their invaluable guidance and suggestions in a project to which they gave their enthusiastic support from the beginning.

Nihil Obstat:
Rev. Msgr. Robert L. Ferring

Imprimatur:
Most Rev. Daniel W. Kucera, O.S.B.
Archbishop of Dubuque

The imprimatur is an official declaration that a book or pamphlet is free of doctrinal or moral error. No implication is contained therein that anyone who granted the Imprimatur agrees with the contents, opinions, or statements expressed.

Fourth printing 1999

Twenty-Third Publications
185 Willow Street
P.O. Box 180
Mystic, CT 06355
(860) 536-2611
(800) 321-0411

ISBN 0-89622-574-7
Library of Congress Catalog Card Number 93-60818
Printed in the U.S.A.

Foreword

When my friend of many years, Ed Macauley, told me that he and Msgr. Francis Friedl were writing a book called *Homilies Alive*, he had my attention. The most powerful messages we hear should be coming from the pulpit every Sunday morning. Much of what I see on television and in the movies no longer supports the lessons the nuns taught me at St. Ambrose Grade School in St. Louis. But I know how tough it is for the homilist to compete with the powerful messages of the popular media. You'd think it would be easy, since the homilist has God's Word to talk about, and no other message comes close to the power and beauty of those words. Yet I hear homilies that don't seem to measure up to those great passages from the Old and New Testaments. Writing and delivering better homilies is what this book is about.

From my own experience of sitting in the Sunday congregation, I know that any number of things can derail what could be a successful homily. Sometimes the homilist fails to relate the Scriptures to daily life. Sometimes he has a good message, but doesn't use the fundamentals that every good speaker uses to make a message come to life. At other times, the homilist gets right up to the point of tackling the hard issues that concern all of us, and just when I think I'm going to hear solid insights about the problems of materialism or dishonesty in business and government, or why my faith isn't as strong as it could be, the homilist backs off and avoids the tough answers. Every once in a while, I hear an excellent ten-minute sermon that's spoiled because the homilist took twenty minutes to deliver it.

Many people say that communicating an interesting, motivating, and even inspiring message is a God-given talent, but that's just not true. If you want to be good at anything, you have to learn the fundamentals, have the courage to try them out, perhaps fail many times, but you keep working at it until you get it right. That's true in baseball, broadcasting, and in speaking to an audience, including the one in church.

Believe me, I know. Early in my broadcasting and public speaking career, I used three-by-five cards to remind me of jokes or baseball stories. Sometimes they got laughs, sometimes they didn't. I listened to other men and women, I learned from them, and I didn't quit when I failed. It's a great thrill to stand before a room full of people and make them feel that what you've said is worthwhile. That's why I envy homilists. They have a great opportunity every Sunday, every day, to change the lives of people, to improve society, and to lead people to God. And they just can't afford to waste those opportunities.

This book will help any homilist reach people with his message. Ed Macauley and Msgr. Friedl get right down to the nitty-gritty. They write about the fundamentals of communicating, starting with a section that tells homilists what they must believe in order to be successful. I especially like the chapter on conversion, in which they explain how a homilist finds meaning in the Scripture readings and applies them to our daily lives. Then comes a section of ten chapters, each discussing one fundamental of speaking that every speaker should know, whether giving a homily or narrating a segment on the "Today" show. For instance, there's a chapter on making sure that the homily is of interest to the people, that it's really going to grab them. It's a very simple idea, but it works. That's what Jesus Christ did: He spoke our language and told it as it was. He spoke in parables—simple stories in simple words. That's what a homilist needs to do. In television, if people aren't interested, they simply change the channel. In church, they use their built-in remote control and tune out.

The chapter on setting goals and objectives is very helpful. Sometimes when I'm listening to a homily I'm wondering where the homilist is going. I'm lost. If I don't know where he is headed, pretty soon I tune him out. If I know where the homilist is headed, we get there together. Otherwise, he makes the trip alone.

The chapter on being specific is also a winner. In television, that's a must. When you watch a commercial, you know exactly what the advertiser wants you to do. Yet sometimes I hear homilies that make me think I'm going to get specific answers to real problems, like fighting temptation or keeping my faith strong, only to hear the homilist wind up with useless generalities. It's a letdown. This book can help you solve that problem. Of course, what makes all these fundamentals come alive is the authors' easy-to-read style and their practical suggestions.

The authors' advice on being yourself is vital. I learned long ago that I can't be anyone else but myself; I'm still a guy from "The Hill," the Italian section of St. Louis. I don't try to come across as a Rhodes scholar. I let my audiences know I sometimes fail and that I'm still trying.

Yes, Ed Macauley got my attention when he told me that he and Msgr. Friedl were working together on *Homilies Alive*. What a combination! A Hall of Fame athlete who fought his way up from being an average player as a boy to be ranked one of the fifty finest basketball players in America, and who spent the greater part of his life in broadcasting; and a priest who has taught at every level from kindergarten to graduate school, and who has preached to children, adults, and scholars. These two spent about three years on this book, from first outline to publication. But I'm glad they took their time, because they've written a practical, readable book that will help any homilist preach better.

In the 1990s we're bombarded with messages opposed to what Jesus teaches us. But his words are as powerful today as they were 2000 years ago. His teachings can stand up to the selfish messages we hear today, especially if the person in the pulpit knows how to communicate with the congregation. I hope every priest, minister, deacon, and seminarian reads this book and keeps it nearby. Once they read it, they'll soon see the folks in the pews looking up in surprise and appreciation for hearing homilies that have really come alive.

Joe Garagiola

Foreword

───────

But how can they call on him in whom they have not believed? And how can they believe in him of whom they have not heard? And how can they hear without someone to preach? (Rom. 10:14)

This passage came to mind when the authors of this remarkable volume on homiletics invited me to write a foreword. Proclaiming the Good News of Salvation has always held the place of primacy in God's church, but never more so than today when the cacophony of a world going in all directions threatens to drown out the prophetic voice.

As I read the manuscript, I became increasingly excited about its possibility for those of us who preach and for those in seminaries who are preparing to proclaim the Gospel of Jesus Christ. This is a book full of practical suggestions and examples. It is especially full of the faith dimension that underlies all preaching and makes it come alive. *Homilies Alive* is indeed an apt title.

Monsignor Francis Friedl and Deacon Edward Macauley have pooled their considerable talents and personal experiences to produce a timely and coherent treatise on the art of preaching. The book aptly begins with the faith dimension of the preacher himself. Again quoting St. Paul: "I determined that while I was with you I would preach of nothing but Jesus Christ and him crucified" (1 Cor. 2:2). Unless the Word Incarnate animates the very life of the preacher, the best of structured homilies may well miss their mark.

The other sections of the book on the content of a homily and the skill of the homilist deal with making effective contact with the hearer to leave a clear and focused message. The Sunday homily competes for the attention of a congregation with hours upon hours of television and media blitzes. There is only a short time during the liturgy to give the Gospel message. The homily must be as effective as the 30-second sound byte so successfully used for mundane advertising. The authors present much material from which to craft such a "sound byte"—the Sunday sermon that will grasp the attention and touch the hearts of the hearers.

It is a pleasure to recommend this volume, particularly so because of my personal knowledge of the life and abilities of the authors. They do not recommend anything other than what they themselves have experienced and used in a lifetime of effective preaching. Those who use this book to shape and hone their craft of preaching God's Word will find it a treasure trove of useful suggestions.

Daniel W. Kucera, O.S.B.
Archbishop of Dubuque

Preface

Many books on homilies have already been written. Why another? We see at least three reasons. First, an increased desire on the part of lay persons for good homilies. The most common criticism of preaching is that homilists neither prepare nor address spiritual issues that affect people's lives. Though many priests work very hard to interpret the Word of God, the general disappointment in the result of their efforts is a fact. In a survey of Catholics in Green Bay (Wisconsin) Diocese, dated Jan. 15, 1993, fewer than one-third (29%) of the respondents felt that Sunday homilies helped them very much in living out their daily lives in their homes. Restricting the replies to those Catholics with children at home, only 21% said that the homily helps them very much in their daily lives.

Second, increased interest among Catholics in Scripture, and a parallel interest and competence among Catholic scholars. These changes open new doors and offer expanded opportunities for homilies that relate Scripture to life experiences. Prior to Vatican II, a principal difference between Catholic and mainline Protestant faiths was the emphasis given to preaching. Protestants stressed Scripture, Catholics stressed sacrament. Since Vatican II the situation has changed, and Catholic scholars are among the leaders in biblical studies. Consequently, Catholic people today view Scripture as the living word of God and are searching for ways to apply it to their daily lives. Programs for catechumens (R.C.I.A.), Renew, and the lay ministry movement have supported the renewed interest in Scripture.

Third, the increased need for the church to address serious contemporary problems, for example, the sense of overriding need for personal fulfillment at the expense of sensitivity to the needs of others, the increasing divorce rate, abortion, the proliferation of AIDS, threats to the environment, sexism, racism, drugs, firearms in the schoolyard, and teenage pregnancy. Not all these issues are new. What is new is their pervasiveness in modern society.

These problems cannot be solved without the development of a deep and living faith in our congregations, a faith that does not simply say, "I believe in all the truths the church teaches," or "I am completely committed to our Savior, Jesus Christ," but a faith that generates in the members of the congregation a conviction that celebrating the Eucharist is the most powerful, most fulfilling, most important event of their day, perhaps of their life. The homilist is obliged not only to guide people toward the solution of moral problems, but also to provide insights that will lead to deepening and maturing their faith. In fact, it is precisely the growth of faith that provides the most effective antidote to most of the problems we have described. In former times, there were many opportunities for instruction that are not available today: catechism classes, a faith-based society, an entertainment industry that recognized spiritual values, the support of governmental leaders. Homilies delivered in those days reinforced beliefs widely accepted. Today, homilies are one of the few societal sources for the development and preservation of Christian faith.

Sometimes a fresh approach will bring about results when traditional solutions are no longer available. Years ago, at Loras Academy in Dubuque, Father Luke Striegel, a deeply spiritual and hard-working priest, would speak to the boarding students on Wednesday nights, the evening scheduled for the sacrament of reconciliation. He was determined to provide a motive for his students to receive the sacrament and would come up with the most unusual types of encouragement. One night he would say, "Today is the feast of a great saint who died a martyr just at your age, a saint who made weekly confession a regular practice." The next week he might explain that the beginning of Lent is a perfect time to settle accounts with the Lord. A week later he would say, "Sunday will be Parents' Day. Everyone should be at communion that day. Confessions will be heard in a few minutes in the chapel." Although he spoke with enthusiasm and conviction, it did not appear likely that his presentations to a group of rather bored teenagers would produce much fruit. Yet, strangely enough, each of his appeals evoked a positive response from one or other group of students, although it had little or no effect on the others. Because he varied his approach each Wednesday, he managed in the long run to reach every student at the Academy. It is our hope that this book will strike a responsive chord in homilists because its approach is somewhat different from previous publications on homiletics.

How is this book unlike other publications? Three differences might be cited. First, the breadth of background of the authors. The book is a collaborative effort between two homilists with distinctly different backgrounds. One is a Hall of Fame basketball player, the other a priest. The more athletic of us has spent thirty years in the field of communications and is a permanent Deacon in the Archdiocese of St. Louis. He sees a direct application to homilies of the insights that helped him gain success in athletics and in the world of radio and television. The priest, also a psychologist, a former pastor, and former college president, has gained valuable insights on preaching through his wide range of experiences during fifty years in the ministry.

A second difference between this and many books on homiletics is that we have not attempted a technical treatise on preaching. There is no historical review of the art of speaking, no development of comprehensive exegeses of the scriptural readings, and no extensive quotation from sources. The book presumes that the preacher has already researched the Scriptures. It is an outline and a discussion of ten fundamentals, a compilation of gleanings from observation, training, and practice that the athlete and the priest judge to be central to the success of homiletic communication in the times we live in.

A third difference is found in the stress on the diversity of individual congregations. The congregation is not a congealed mass of heads with a unified character. We have built on an age-old principle of rhetoric that the congregation, like any audience, consists of many individuals who at any given moment hold significantly varying interests, needs, and types of motivation. Our book explores why and how the homilist can use that fact to make his homilies hit the mark with most members of the congregation.

Archbishop Kucera, in his Foreword, has correctly identified the two fundamental requisites for effectively proclaiming the Good News: 1) the presence of a vibrant faith life in the preacher, and 2) the skills needed to deliver a clear and focused message. We completely concur with that statement. However, this publication is chiefly directed to the second of these requisites, namely, to help the preacher acquire the skills needed for successful communication.

If priests, ministers, and deacons will profit in some way, if they will touch their congregations a bit more deeply because of what we have written, our efforts will be worthwhile.

For the most part we have relied on our personal experiences and those of our colleagues to describe our ideas. Occasionally we have invented examples that help illustrate a point. In most of these we use the simple technique of placing the examples, both real and invented, in a hypothetical but typical parish with named characters. Any similarity to persons living or dead is purely coincidental and unintended. We think you will often recognize some of our characters by merely changing a name.

Note: The book itself is a combination of the experiences and insights of the two authors, most of them shared. However, some past experiences of each are unique and should be so identified. Rather than let the reader guess whose chronicle is being related at any given point, we identify the source by placing the initials (FF for Francis Friedl, and EM for Ed Macauley) at the beginning of each specific personal contribution.

Contents

DEDICATION

To the many priests, deacons, and ministers
who love the task of preaching
and who spend the best part of the week preparing their homilies,
aware of both the awesome responsibility
and the unique privilege which is theirs.
May their numbers increase.

Part One

What the Homilist Must Believe

The Fundamentals of Communication Make Homilies Come Alive

Do you dread writing homilies? Do you find the obligation of composing a homily for the weekend congregation a drudgery? Are you relieved when it is the turn for the associate pastor or for one of the parish deacons to give the homily? When it is your turn to preach, do you put off writing the homily until Friday evening or even Saturday morning? If your answer is yes to any of these questions, you need to become convinced that the most important thing a priest, deacon, or minister does during the entire week is not the visitation of the sick, not counseling the bereaved, but the proclamation of the Word of God. In Chapter 2 we shall discuss the importance of the homily.

Do your parishioners find it difficult to relate to the scriptural readings at the weekday or Sunday liturgies? At weddings and funerals, do members of your congregation suggest readings from Kahlil Gibran or Malcolm X, instead of the recommended scriptural passages? If the answer is yes, perhaps you have failed to convert the messages of the Old and New Testaments to the lives of your people. Perhaps you have neglected to show them in your homilies how these writings, jotted down on parchment some 3000 years ago, still speak with freshness and perceptivity of human wants and needs and dreams. Chapter 3 outlines the process of biblical conversion that will make Sacred Scripture relevant to your parishioners.

Are your homilies sharp, concise, and effective? Is your congregation silent and attentive during the delivery of your message? As you look out at the congregation, do you often see a nod of the head or a smile indicating that you have just struck a responsive chord? If your answer is no, perhaps you need to study and practice the fundamentals of homiletic communication which we describe in Chapters 4 through 13. The world is full of golfers, perhaps including you, all of whom are constantly trying to improve their scores. They seek tips from the golf magazines, ask counsel from their low-handicap friends, and eventually take lessons from their club pro. No matter how amateur or experienced the student, every competent golf pro will begin the instruction by addressing the basic fundamentals of the game: the grip, the setup, and the swing. The homilist who is unsure of the effectiveness of his presentations should begin the same way—with the fundamentals of homiletic communication.

The Fundamentals

You are standing in the pulpit and doing your very best to deliver a cogent and acceptable homily. Then you notice with exasperation that the congregation is simply not listening. Mrs. Jackman, probably the most pious woman in the parish, is saying her rosary. Jack Sheridan, right up front, is reading the fascinating chronicles of the Sunday bulletin. The two McFadden tykes are chasing Cheerios across the floor. Somewhere babies are crying. And your most reliable ushers, Norm and Ralph, are whispering their strategy for taking up the collection. Would the situation be any different if your message was applied to daily experiences and problems that are of deep *interest* to these and all the members of your congregation? Is it possible that you have not *prepared and organized* your homily thoroughly?

You have finished your homily and later visit with the lay ministers in the sacristy. You are hoping they will be excited about your message, that they will speak of ways in which they plan to carry out the suggestions for action you have made in the homily, but their feedback is vague and uncertain. There seems to be no change in your parishioners as a result of the messages you deliver. Were you *specific* in your presentation? Did you omit taking a step that is important for many homilies, the *call for action*? Did you forget to identify a *goal* and a *specific objective* for your homily?

At a Monday evening meeting of the Liturgy Committee you ask the early-comers to summarize what you said in the pulpit. They come up with a potpourri of eight or ten different interpretations of your message. Are you sure that you restricted your homily to a *single topic*?

Does one segment of your congregation seem to respond to your message, while the rest consistently ignore what you are saying or suggesting? Perhaps you have failed to include in your homily *as many members of the congregation as possible*.

Mary and Joe Massey relate well with you when you visit them in their home, but they seem distant and unresponsive when you are giving a homily. You might ask yourself whether you are *being yourself* in the pulpit. Are you coming across to them as two different persons? Is one of them the friendly pastor who enjoys visiting with them during the week, eager to learn about their children, the progress of their business, and their plans for the future; the other, a distant, pompous orator who speaks on an entirely different level when in the pulpit?

Does the congregation exhibit interest during the first part of the homily, but seem to drift away toward the end? Does Jay Frank, the banker, or Tom Cawley, the insurance broker, sometimes suggest, very delicately, that the liturgy seems to be stretched out a little? Take a close look at the *timing* of your presentation.

Does outspoken Blanche Carr, or Bud Ferring, of letters-to-the-editor fame, sometimes come up to you after your homily and differ with you, present another viewpoint, or even express anger at what you have said? Was your reaction one of having failed in the pulpit? Do you look at a "successful" homily as one that elicits total support of the entire congregation? Providing, of course, that the homily was in good taste and was not needlessly offensive, you should be pleased with that kind of response; at least they were listening. Perhaps you have not accepted the fact that a much needed, hard-hitting, homily that every speaker must occasionally deliver will inevitably arouse opposition, that every successful homilist must expect, at times, *disagreement and failure*.

If any of these scenarios are a part of your Sunday liturgy, then you need to go back to the basics. We have just identified above ten fundamentals we believe are vital in developing the art of competent homiletic communication. Our conviction is that careful study and application of these fundamentals will add to the style and quality of every speaker, even those who are convinced that they have little natural talent for preaching. The sustained and intelligent use of these fundamentals will make your homilies come alive. Here is the list of the fundamentals, each of which will be developed in a subsequent chapter.

1. The homily should be of interest to the congregation.
2. The homily should have a recognizable goal and objective.
3. The homily should have a single topic.
4. The homily should be specific.
5. The homily should ask for specific action.
6. The homily should speak to the entire congregation.
7. You must time your homily properly.
8. You must prepare and organize your homily.
9. You must be yourself to be believable.
10. You must expect occasional disagreement and failure.

Elements of Successful Communication

There are three elements involved in the delivery of compelling communication of any kind: 1) good technique (the proper use of voice, gestures, visual aids, etc.); 2) the ability to recognize and respond to the needs of the audience; 3) most important of all, a meaningful message.

Arsenio Hall and Jay Leno have great technique. They make extensive use of self-deprecation, they are masters of the one-liner, and their sense of timing is superb.

The television evangelists have something that goes beyond technique. They have developed an extraordinary ability to recognize and respond to the needs of today's audiences. They attract an astonishing number of people to the auditoriums where they speak and among home viewers. Their appeal is measured not only by the multitudes who listen to them, but by the very large sums of money contributed by the millionaire and the lowest wage earner. The power and income of the evangelists, vaguely suspected for some years, were brought to light only with the court case against the Bakkers. A priest who recently gave a workshop on homilies in the Dubuque Archdiocese stated that he watched Jimmy Swaggart preach on a given weekend, and was "mesmerized" by the strength of his appeal. What lies behind the force exerted by the television evangelist on the viewers and the audience? It is certainly not the message, for with a few exceptions (Billy Graham is one) the message is almost devoid of sound theology and full of platitudes. But they are masters at putting their finger on the hungers of the ordinary person: the need to be stroked; the need to feel wanted, safe, and saved; the need for simple answers to complex questions. They have a facility for applying the words of Scripture to the interests and concerns of their congregations. No matter that the interpretations may be strained and at times incorrect, they are able to tap the deepest needs of their viewers and respond to them in religious terms.

The talk show hosts are masters of technique; television evangelists are skillful at identifying human needs and applying them to scriptural texts. For both, though, the message is the least important of the three elements of successful communication. For the serious homilist, the message comes first. There is no more effective and compelling message in the universe than the Good News of the Gospel. It is a story related by the heavenly Father, telling us we are children of God and that we are loved no matter what our transgressions; it is a proclamation of Jesus, revealing that he has redeemed us because he knew and loved us before we were conceived; it is a revelation from the Holy Spirit, the same word of truth and goodness that lit a fire under the timid apostles on the first Christian Pentecost.

Precisely because the homilist *begins* with such a message, he has a great advantage over other kinds of speakers. No other communicator can compete with the power of that message, deeply believed and capably delivered. Technique can be learned, the ability to recognize needs can be developed, but nothing can surpass the depth and beauty and power of the message that is the basis of every homily.

When we step into the pulpit, we are in competition with every other communicator the congregation has seen or heard during the past week. Some of them are superb: Leno, Hall, Swaggart, Eddie Murphy, Phil Donahue, Oprah Winfrey, and many others. Although the message we proclaim has stacked the odds in our favor, our congregations will not automatically view our presentations as in a category distinct from other messages they hear daily. If we are, in fact, in a contest with such masters of communication, we must adopt and use the tried and proven techniques of the television specialists. We must use every skill and technique of delivery that can make a communication attractive. We must study and discern and respond to the concerns and needs of the people as capably as the television evangelists and comedians. Careful application of the suggestions in this book will provide the homilist with the skills needed to do this.

There are two additional factors working for us that are not always available to public speakers: 1) we have the good will and faith of the people because of our ministry, and 2) we are not obliged to use promos or advance teams to ensure attendance at weekend Masses. A captive audience is a benefit rarely given to other speakers.

If we really believe we have a message more powerful than that delivered by the great communicators who successfully bombard us with less significant themes, then we have the capacity to be dynamic communicators of God's Word. If we are convinced that this capacity can be enhanced by refining our techniques of delivery and our ability to recognize and respond to the needs of our congregation, there can be no excuse for inadequate preaching.

No homilist need approach the pulpit with trepidation. Christ promised: "I will be with you all days." But the effectiveness of his assistance depends on our willingness to learn and use all of our experience, talent, and ability to maximize our skills. Walter Burghardt says in *Preaching: The Art and the Craft:* "I do not minimize divine inspiration; I simply suggest it is rarely allotted to the lazy" (p. 10). By the lazy, he meant those who are unwilling to develop the expertise of effective homiletic communication that is available to anyone willing to spend a reasonable amount of time and energy.

There is still another factor that favors the homilist. As ordained clergy, priests and deacons have a special calling, a sacramental calling, to proclaim the Word of the Lord to the assembly. That gift should enable us to make God's Word a living, enthralling message. It is a source of extra power, giving us still another edge in our communication. But even with this sacramental help, success in delivering the Sunday message is predicated on a mastery, at whatever level we can reach, of the fundamentals of homiletic communication.

— 2 —

Homilies Are Vitally Important

God is present at the liturgy both in Word and in Sacrament. The Eucharist has been the very center of our faith and devotion from the beginning of Christianity. Yet for several reasons many members of our congregations, especially the children, do not seem to have the same understanding of and enthusiasm for the Eucharist as in earlier days. That enthusiasm needs rekindling. One of the best ways to build a love for the Eucharist is through the preaching of excellent homilies that have a message for every age group. We shall attempt to point out how to prepare and deliver such homilies through the use of the fundamentals of homiletic communication.

Before examining the fundamentals, it is appropriate to ask a basic question: "How important *are* homilies?" Is the homily simply a portion of the liturgy that had meaning as an educational exercise in days past when higher learning was reserved to the clergy and civic leaders and when access to books was limited? Or does the homily still play an important, even an essential, part in our community worship, with potentially profound effects on our daily lives?

The People of God
Our conviction is that homilies are vitally important. First of all, in our experience the *congregation* judges that the homily is a very

important part of the liturgy. One of the genuine surprises in store for the newly ordained priest and deacon is the reaction of the people to his messages. Because the homilist receives little immediate feedback from the congregation, and because the homily is both mandatory and regular, the assumption is often made that the people in the pews have a "ho-hum" attitude toward it. "We have to listen to it, so let's get it over with so we can get on with the important part of the liturgy."

Very few members of the congregation have this attitude. Never in our memory have so many people approached the priest or deacon after a particularly good homily and offered their congratulations—and thanks, a reaction seldom conveyed to other public speakers. Their response to the homily is not affected politeness, but a sincere expression of appreciation for something they value. Their gratitude is prompted by their awareness of what the preacher has done for them by the careful preparation and delivery of his message. They are a captive audience. Most of them come for the liturgy of the Eucharist—not for the homily—but when they hear a homily that affects their daily experience, the value of their worship has been enhanced. The well-prepared homilist declares his respect for the congregation, his realization of the value of their time, as well as his commitment to deepening their spiritual values.

The gratitude of the congregation for an excellent homily comes from a second source: an extraordinary kindling of interest in Sacred Scripture among the average members of the congregation, that is, among those with no special training in biblical studies. Thirty years ago, if a pastor gave his parishioners a list of opportunities for group discussion, Bible study would have come in last. Today the study of Scripture has a high priority. Scripture reflection is common in meetings of parish councils, boards of education, and small Christian communities; it forms the backbone of the sessions of spiritual life committees, charismatic gatherings, and most parish programs directed to the spiritual growth of the parishioners. One can sense in every congregation a genuine craving to hear the Word of God explained, interpreted, and applied to the problems the members face at home, in the office, and in the community.

What has caused such a remarkable resurgence of interest in

Sacred Scripture? Two events in the recent history of the church stand out as at least partly responsible. One is the 1943 encyclical *Divino Afflante Spiritu* of Pope Pius XII, which permitted, for the first time, exploration and study of Scripture through the use of the modern tools of literary criticism, and which gave impetus to the rapid expansion of Catholic biblical scholarship in this century. The second is the 1965 *Dogmatic Constitution on Divine Revelation* of Vatican Council II, which encourages reading of the Bible by the faithful, and stresses biblical faith as being loyal adherence to a personal God, rather than intellectual assent to a group of propositions. These two historic documents are of particular interest to the clergy, opening for them broad vistas of biblical scholarship; but the results of that scholarship have also provided for the laity a deeper understanding of the Scriptures.

Still another source for renewed interest of Scripture among the laity is their natural hunger for guidance concerning the complex moral issues of the day: divorce, broken homes, abortion, dishonesty at all levels, the rape of the environment. The failure of so many self-styled prophets to offer satisfactory answers to these issues has led many of the faithful to a realization that answers must be found in Sacred Scripture, in the teachings of Jesus Christ.

Homilists often say that we are living in a difficult time for preaching. The opposite is true. When the forces of evil are prevailing is precisely the time that people are most eager to hear a message that can blunt those forces. Yes, it *is* a difficult time to preach if we don't have the answers to the spiritual needs of our congregations, and if we are unable to communicate those answers successfully. But it is a very rewarding time to preach if we do have both the solutions and the knowledge of how to communicate those solutions. If the homilist is not convinced that the teachings of Jesus provide a basis for answers to all our spiritual needs, he should stay out of the pulpit.

The Clergy

Homilies, then, are important to the congregation. They are also important to the official leadership of the church. If you were asked which is your first duty, to proclaim the Word of God or to celebrate the sacraments, how would you respond? If you say "to celebrate the sacraments," we would remind you of the 1965 *Decree on the Ministry and Life of Priests* of Vatican II, which states that "Priests, as co-workers with their bishops, have as their *primary duty the proclamation of the Gospel of God to all*" (Chapter II, section 4, emphasis added). And so, while the eucharistic celebration is the most sacred of all Christian actions and the basis of all worship for the Christian community, the first *duty* of the priest and deacon is to proclaim God's Word in every possible way, especially through the Liturgy of the Word during the celebration of Mass.

In a booklet published by the Bishops' Committee on Priestly Life and Ministry (*Fulfilled in Your Hearing: The Homily in the Sunday Assembly*. U.S. Catholic Conference, 1982, p. 1), the bishops comment on this statement of the Council:

These clear, straightforward words of the Second Vatican Council may still come as something of a surprise to us. We might more spontaneously think the primary duty of priests is the celebration of the church's sacraments, or pastoral care of the People of God, or the leadership of the Christian Community. Yet, the words of the document are clear: the proclamation of the Gospel is primary. The other duties of the priests are to be considered properly presbyteral to the degree they support the proclamation of the Gospel. . . . A key moment in the proclamation of the Gospel is preaching, preaching which is characterized by "proclamation of God's wonderful works in the history of salvation. . . ." We also recognize that for the vast majority of Catholics, the Sunday homily is the normal and frequently the formal way in which they hear the Word of God proclaimed. For these Catholics the Sunday homily may well be the most decisive factor in determining the depth of their faith and strengthening the level of their commitment to the church.

To find a more official and a clearer declaration of the primary task of the priest would be difficult. In the statement of the bishops, saying that the Sunday homily is the "normal and frequently the formal" way in which people hear the Word of God, they might well have added "and the *only* way in which they hear God's words." The messages we receive from television, radio, and talk show personalities are almost totally materialistic. If we do not bring scriptural applications to the lives of our people, who will?

Society

There has been a radical and far-reaching change in the times we are now living, compared to just a generation ago. Formerly, society supported the teachings of Christianity; so did the leaders of society. Today the social forces that once bolstered the doctrines of the church have weakened considerably, and all too often our leaders reflect those forces instead of trying to direct and shape them. What, for example, would have been the result of a Gallup Poll twenty years ago asking whether marital fidelity should be an important consideration in the election of persons for public office, or whether condoms should be distributed in high schools? Actually, such polls were rarely taken years ago by responsible agencies. The results would have been obvious. Because social pressures reinforcing Christian teaching have almost disappeared, the homilist is frequently called upon to assume the role of the Old Testament prophet: to speak out against both society and its leaders when they do not support Yahweh's commandments.

Being Practical

During the course of an average week the priest meets with perhaps twenty or thirty individuals for spiritual discussions or parish business. He will visit another ten or twenty in the hospital. He will touch still another fifty or a hundred through meetings with parish organizations. All of these contacts may consume thirty to forty hours at a minimum. By contrast, on Sunday he will reach the entire listening congregation, 500 or 1000 or more, depending on the parish size, and will have approximately ten to fifteen minutes to deliver his message through the homily. These are the most precious, most potentially effective, minutes he will spend during the entire week. They are not spent on matters of business or finance or school or construction, but on spiritual issues. The congregation is eager to hear the Word of God and learn new insights concerning problems of their spiritual life from someone committed to reflecting on God's communication to us through the Scriptures.

From a standpoint of pure efficiency, those ten to fifteen minutes should be the most carefully prepared, thoroughly studied portion of the week. From the standpoint of personal satisfaction, they should be the most enjoyable and rewarding moments of the ministry. If the homilist speaks for ten minutes to a thousand people, he is communicating the Word of God for ten thousand minutes, or 166 hours, almost a week. Thus what began as ten minutes for the homilist is expanded into nearly an entire week of communication to the congregation.

Other reasons might be listed to underscore the prominence that homilies should play in the life of priest, minister, and deacon, but the reader who has come to this point in the book is already convinced of the need for quality homiletic communication and is looking for answers and methods, not further demonstration of an accepted fact.

If the claim for the importance of preaching is demonstrably valid, why are homilies not as effective as the congregation would wish them to be? One reason may be that we are all still a bit tainted by the old theological principle of *ex opere operato*. If the Mass is said to produce its effect automatically without any particular input from the celebrant, why try to gild the lily?

Perhaps, too, there is a lingering effect of the emphasis the church once placed on sacrament at the expense of preaching the Word. Most Protestant denominations place less stress than do Catholics on the eucharistic portion of the liturgy. Consequently, it is most important for them to do a very creditable job in preaching. Often the Catholic homilist does not feel the same obligation.

Possibly the primary reason for ineffective preaching is that many homilists are not aware of, or do not review constantly, the fundamentals of oral communication. Our book is addressed to this last item. So often, priests, ministers, and deacons judge that talent, skill, and ability in speaking are natural gifts. If you don't have them, there is nothing you can do about it. That is no more true in the area of preaching than it is in athletics.

EM: I played on an eighth-grade basketball team that did not win a game. I did not play as a freshman in high school and was the substitute center on the sophomore team at St. Louis

University High School. Natural talent offered no avenue to success at this point. But then I began my journey to the Basketball Hall of Fame by learning the basics and constantly practicing them, three hours every day.

Those who succeed in any job are the ones who have mastered the fundamentals of their profession. People are not merely "gift-ed." Deacon Clarence Enzler, of Washington, D.C., was one of the finest speakers in the country. He did not come by it naturally. He was born with a severe speech defect and stuttered constantly. He worked many hours and long days to overcome this defect; he practiced over and over several of the basic elements of oral communication. Eventually, in the 1960s, he took first place in the national toastmaster contest for extemporaneous after-dinner speaking.

In Chapters 4 through 13, we shall present and discuss each of the fundamentals listed in Chapter 1. These fundamentals are essential to developing the art of competent homiletic communication. Careful study and application of these simple principles will add to the style and quality of every speaker.

— 3 —

Biblical Conversion Paves the Way to Effective Homilies

Every homily, by definition, involves the application of Sacred Scripture to the issues and problems facing the people in the pews. There are two principal methods of making Scripture understandable to the congregation: 1) expounding on the *literal* sense of the passage, as intended by the human author, 2) interpreting Scripture by using one of the *more-than-literal* senses of the passage.

The Literal Sense

Bible study courses describe the historical, social, political, and religious background of a particular pericope so that students will realize what the passage meant to the people living when the biblical book was written. This method of study seeks to determine the literal sense of selected passages, that is, the meaning intended by the book's author. The technique serves a useful purpose when research and education are the goals of the process, and is particularly effective for those with some background and training in hermeneutics. When used in a homily, such information should be confined to the introductory portion of the message. The purpose of the preacher is not to teach a class, but to make Sacred Scripture come alive for the congregation.

More-than-Literal Senses

A function of biblical interpretation of equal importance to the understanding of Scripture, one that is more helpful toward the construction of an effective homily, is that of determining the significance of scriptural passages beyond the basic meaning of the author. Scripture scholars identify several of these senses: 1) *the new hermeneutic*, which is more concerned with what Scripture says to a person living in the twentieth century than with what it meant when it was written; 2) the *Christian interpretation of Scripture*, which seeks to define an interrelationship between the two testaments, partly through emphasizing how Old Testament prophecies are fulfilled in Christianity; and 3) the *sensus plenior*, which concentrates on the deeper meaning intended by God, but not clearly sensed or intended by the human author. (For a discussion of these meanings of Scripture, see Raymond E. Brown, "Hermeneutics," *Jerome Biblical Commentary*, pp. 605-23.)

Still another method of relating Scripture to daily life is called *accommodation*. Much of the exegesis of the Fathers of the church, including Chrysostom, Ambrose, Gregory, and Augustine, made extensive use of accommodation, a form of interpretation which, although useful in some cases, often goes beyond the generally accepted more-than-literal senses, and involves the preacher's personal application to circumstances which were not envisioned by the original authors. Brown ("Hermeneutics," p. 619) gives this example of accommodation: Gregory the Great tells his audience that the Gospel parable of the five talents refers to the five senses. Another use of accommodation: The liturgy applies to the lives of popes and bishops the words Sirach (45:24) uses to praise Phinehas, son of Eleazar: "The Lord sealed a covenant of peace with him, and made him a prince, bestowing the priestly dignity upon him for ever."

Biblical Conversion

We use the term "biblical conversion" for the process of applying scriptural passages to the common experiences of congregation members. To convert means to change to another form or substance, to transform. In biblical conversion, the form or the message of the scriptural passage is changed by applying it to circumstances of today's world. The message remains the same, but it is converted to include up-to-date terminology and to make applications to issues familiar to the congregation. Biblical conversion allows the congregation to understand the message in the same way it was understood by those who first heard it. Both literal exegesis and biblical conversion are helpful in the development of a homily but, generally speaking, literal exegesis should be confined to the preparation of the homilist, as background to his understanding of the meaning of that portion of Scripture. Biblical conversion is nearly identical with the new hermeneutic, but the term "conversion" is, in our judgment, more meaningful to the average homilist. Biblical conversion, like the new hermeneutic, is several steps above accommodation, a use of Scripture that is closer to being a product of the homilist's imagination than of the Scripture author's original intent.

Sand and water mixed together are not an effective composite for the foundation of a building. But if you add cement, you have converted those two elements to concrete. A river rushing through a gorge is not particularly useful to our way of life; dam it, convert it to electricity, and you have made the stream into a product that will light homes and run factories. Apple seeds have little value in themselves. Plant them into the ground and add moisture, and you have converted them to a tree that will produce fruit. That is what you do with a homily. You add the conversion factor, which applies the Scripture passages to the daily concerns of people, and produces something useful and meaningful to the congregation. To bring about this result, you must change, convert, many of the things said by Paul and Matthew and Luke, and even passages from the Old Testament, to something concrete and significant to your listeners.

If you are using the Parable of the Good Samaritan, the literal application to present-day circumstances would suggest that, in order for you to be a modern Good Samaritan, you must take the wounded man found by the roadside to a Holiday Inn and pay his bill. The process of biblical conversion would permit the homilist to apply the parable to anyone who is in need physically, emotionally, or even financially. At the funeral of a man named John, who was generous to his neighbors, although not particularly noted for his sanctity of life, the homilist who called him a Good

Samaritan would be using biblical conversion. If the homilist went further and eulogized the man by applying to him the words of John 1:6, "There was a man sent by God whose name was John," he would be making use of accommodation in a fashion that strains the limits of meaning of the original text.

Average members of the congregation do not have the educational background to profit by the literal interpretation of Scripture, nor are they interested in Old Testament texts supporting the divinity of Christ. But each one does have an interest in what the Word of God means for him or her in the circumstances in which he or she lives. Parishioners wish to know how that Word can bring them and their children closer to the Lord. Conversion is especially meaningful for teenagers and young married couples. It is also important for golden-agers who for perhaps the first time in their lives are beginning to come to a full realization that their time on Earth may be running out.

The booklet of the Bishops' Committee on Priestly Life and Ministry captures well the limitations of literal exegesis used in a homily (*Fulfilled in Your Hearing*, p. 24).

> The very structure of some homilies gives the impression that the preacher's principal purpose is to interpret scriptural texts rather than communicate with real people, and he interprets these texts primarily to extract ethical demands to impose on the congregation. Such preachers may offer good advice, but they are rarely heard as preachers of good news and this very fact distances them from their listeners.

Biblical conversion opens up new meanings of Scripture. The Good Shepherd becomes:

> Eighteen-year-old Sam, who doesn't drink at the party and then says, "I'm sober, so I'll drive home." He may be shepherding the lives of three or four people.

> Kathy, who begins her meal in the restaurant by saying grace, and whose example leads others there to imitate her, at least in their homes.

Ellen, Jane's mother, who has the courage to say, "No, you will not attend the R-rated movie, even if the parents of everyone else say it is OK. I love you too much to allow you to harm yourself."

Edna and Jim, the volunteers who change the missalettes at the end of the month or who offer their services for the various ministries of the weekend liturgy.

Al and Mable, who visit the sick and the aging in hospitals and convalescent homes.

The father of the prodigal son becomes:
Mel, who grieves because his eldest, Matt, is a drug addict, has AIDS, or is an alcoholic, but still shows love and support. The father who is supportive, though disappointed, when his unmarried daughter says, "Daddy, I'm pregnant."

Janet, who forgives her son John unconditionally and not with the comment, "I told you so."

The Good Samaritan becomes:
Henry, the teenage boy who attends a party and engages everyone in conversation, including those girls who are popular and those who are not.

The opera-loving mother who, when driving with teenagers, starts the car and says, "Shall we listen to one of the rock radio stations?"

Dave Brady, owner of The Store for Men, who offers an alcoholic employee an opportunity to participate in AA without leaving his job.

Amanda, who suggests to Louise that they attend Mass together on the anniversary of the death of Louise's husband.

The Sermon on the Mount says:
You are truly a peacemaker when you set an example for every-

one practicing integration by inviting members of a minority family to your home.

You hunger and thirst after justice when you conscientiously study the philosophy of political candidates and then vote for those whose moral and ethical principles agree with Christ's.

The investor becomes poor in spirit when he or she is willing to start a business in or near the ghetto. The primary reason for starting the business is to make a profit, but the secondary reason can be to provide employment for the genuinely poor.

You are merciful when you wipe out an unpayable debt owed to you, and explain to the debtor the biblical reason for your action.

At this point you should try an interesting exercise. Leaf through the New Testament, and take short passages or even sentences, then convert the meaning the words had in Christ's time to those that relate directly to your congregation.

Preparing for the Liturgy

Once the parishioners begin to hear down-to-earth applications of Scripture, once they have had the intriguing experience of seeing how the messages of 2000 and more years ago are living, current, contemporary guides to modern living, the next step is to lead them to read the Bible daily, and especially to prepare for the Sunday liturgy by reading the Scriptures for the day and making their own biblical conversion. There are passages every week which, applied to current situations, can inspire, console, motivate, and warn.

Miss Nixon, an eighth-grade teacher, might read the passage referring to the loaves and fishes, and begin to realize that she can use loaves (education) and fishes (experience) and follow Christ's example of multiplying gifts by educating hundreds of young people in her town.

Ed, a carpenter, or Sally, a clerk, or Jerry, a truck driver, or Phil, a cashier, or anyone who works for a daily wage begins to understand that he or she represents the laborer in the vineyard who arrived at the final hour and received the same compensation as those who had worked much longer. And that realization might inspire gratitude to God for gifts to the working man or woman who is blessed in comparison with workers in China, Mexico, and South America.

Fifteen-year-old Bob and seventeen-year-old Marie could relate to Jesus at the temple when his parents began the journey home only to realize they had left him behind. Jesus and his parents exchanged words indicating that he was becoming aware of his mission in life and of his independence. Yet, as important as that mission was, he subjected himself to his parents' direction and understood the wisdom of responding to their guidance.

All of us could be inspired with Christ's agony in the garden. We resist making the sacrifices involved in following his teachings. We wonder if we are worthy because we have so little faith. And yet, Christ himself says to the Father, not once but three times: "Let this cup pass from me." The human Jesus did not want to undergo the passion. Who could blame him? But when he realized he had to, what a magnificent job he did. How consoling to realize that he found the prospect of dying to save us a difficult undertaking. Our road toward salvation is also difficult, but even though we say "Let this cup pass from me," we can follow up as Christ did by also saying, "Not my will, but yours be done."

In every passage of Scripture, especially in the New Testament, we find examples of how God's Word applies to our lives today. As the pious Mrs. Jackman, the ushers Norm and Ralph, the young Masseys, and the rest of the congregation begin to understand the relevance of those words when they prepare for the Sunday liturgy, homilies will become more meaningful to them. Biblical conversion is the key, and its regular and intelligent use by the homilist is an important step in the development of effective homilies. Look for the relevant meanings, and you will find applications that are simple, compassionate, and loving.

Part Two

What the Homily Should Be Like

— 4 —

Whose Life Are You Dealing With?

The homily should be of interest to the congregation

In the first chapter, we identified ten fundamentals of effective preaching, basic elements that apply to every type of oral communication, including homilies. We rank as number one, as the first fundamental: The message of the homilist should be of interest to the listeners. A simple fact of human nature is that people listen to what interests them; they tune out that which does not.

Getting Their Attention

The initial task of the homilist is to secure the attention of the congregation, but it is not always easy. Many things compete for their attention: the sight of the McFadden tykes in the next pew, tugging at their mother's skirt; the sounds of people shifting in their seats, trying to be comfortable in pews designed for the fifteenth century; the impending due date of the mortgage on the house; Jim's report card from school; and a host of others. In addition, the attention span of the modern American has been shortened considerably by the rapid pace of contemporary life and the compression of radio and TV presentations into finely tuned sound bytes. All the important plays of a baseball game can be condensed into a 20-second video. During periods of inactivity in a game the viewer may switch channels, but not during the highlights. During a homily, the listener whose interest lags will turn to another channel.

How can the homilist overcome such formidable obstacles to attention? First, by presenting a topic that is of vital interest to the listeners. Second, by delivering a credible message, one that corresponds with the way the average member of the congregation views the world.

Speaking to the Congregation's Interests

Parishioners are interested in those things that have a direct bearing on their lives and their loved ones', now and in the future. If you were to jot down at random what things preoccupy you—your everyday concerns, hopes, dreams, and worries—you will find that a surprisingly high percentage of your interests are exactly the same as those of everyone else. Some concerns are specific to particular age groups or to those who share the same occupation, but there is a basic core that is shared by every person.

Universal Interests

Everyone cares about personal health, good appearance, security, material luxuries, acceptance by and respect from others, happiness, freedom, and accomplishing something worthwhile in life. Those with spiritual convictions are also concerned about a greater understanding of how God works in their lives, how Christ's teaching relates to everyday experiences, how they can fulfill his injunction to love their neighbor, and how to achieve eternal happiness.

Particular Interests

In addition to interests that motivate everyone, there are interests specific to various categories of people.

Age groups. Each age group has its own special interests and concerns. Young people are attentive to relations with parents and siblings, peer pressure, appearance, popularity, sports, narcotics, and personal finances.

When they marry, other interests emerge: having children, changing jobs, relocating, losing a job, choosing a school for their children, unwanted pregnancy, remarriage, remaining moral in a competitive business environment, going to church.

As they reach age thirty to forty the most frequent concerns relate to children. How to finance their college education; how to communicate with adolescents; how to deal with their exposure to drugs, alcohol, and sex; raising children as a single parent; and the existence of God.

Those in later years face problems of burnout, change of life, difficulties with married children, health (now a critical factor), missed occupational opportunities, changing careers. In the twilight of life there is a different set of considerations: money for retirement, cost of nursing home care, becoming a widow or widower, neighborhood crime, volunteering to serve others, God's forgiveness.

Occupations give a special focus to problems. Are the listeners union members, lawyers, doctors, attorneys, teachers, farmers? The Scripture passage "What does it profit a man to gain the whole world and suffer the loss of his soul?" will not have the same meaning for all. For the laborer, the quotation will have significance if it is rephrased "Does it really profit me to steal equipment from the shop?" For the professional, "What does it profit me to use unethical practices to advance in my field and earn a fortune?" For the farmer, "To get a higher yield, will I use pesticides that pollute Earth?" For the business person, "Shall I profit at the expense of my employees?" For the salesperson, "Will I sacrifice my integrity by selling shoddy merchandise or give bad advice to make big commissions?" For the student, "Is my life better because I have cheated on exams, told lies to my parents, or slept late and missed Mass on Sunday?"

Special groups. In our country especially, women have assumed increasing responsibility politically and economically. A few of the particular concerns of women are equality in the marketplace, sexual harassment, caring for a handicapped child, blending a career with raising a family, and single parenthood. Racial groups have special interests. Single adults, the handicapped, the divorced, the chemically dependent—all have unique goals to be addressed.

A homilist seldom faces a completely homogeneous congregation. On almost every occasion his audience will include people of several age groups, occupation levels, political affiliations, and avocations. All can be effectively addressed if the homilist directs some portion of his material to at least several of the groups present. Even a single example applicable to children in a homily geared to adults will stimulate the interests of the younger members of the congregation; on feast days such as Christmas, no adult will object to the homilist speaking directly and almost entirely to the children. A word or phrase recognizing the different components of the congregation will let them know their presence has been recognized. The homilist must include every possible group in his audience or risk losing their attention.

Playing the Crowd

There is a phrase used by public entertainers: "Play the crowd." The phrase refers to the technique of finding out who is in the audience and directing the dialogue to them. As a homilist, you have a similar task, and it should be your starting point. When a homily is delivered, here are basic questions you must ask and answer:

1. What are the ages of the congregation?
2. What is their socio-economic condition?
3. What is their educational experience?
4. Are persons of other faiths present?
5. Are there any recent occurrences in the parish, nation, or world that are uppermost in the minds of the congregation?
6. Are there special needs of the persons present?

Funerals and weddings provide special opportunities for healing, for instruction, and for growth in faith. Some liturgists assert that the funeral message must be a totally scriptural homily, a prescription that prevents practically any personal comments on the life of the deceased. We do not subscribe to such a limited concept. The funeral is a time for letting go, but a time when the letting go has not yet taken place. The most frequent and saddest lament expressed after the funeral by grieving relatives is "Father didn't even seem to know who Dad was."

Weddings provide an opportunity both to give instruction on the sacramentality of marriage and to elevate the congregation's respect for an institution that has often been ridiculed and made light of in the entertainment field. Father Al, who is very busy, has used the same homily for the past two dozen couples. As well prepared as that homily may be, it cannot possibly address the needs and interests of every couple and every congregation.

We have given examples of considerations to keep in mind for funerals and weddings. The need to analyze the congregation and identify its interests is equally important for the Saturday evening Mass, the Sunday morning or evening Mass, and the Mass for children.

Applying the Scripture

Having analyzed the congregation, your next step is to determine how the Scripture readings of the liturgy can, in accordance with correct theology, apply to the needs and interests you have identified. This should not be difficult, especially in the New Testament readings, because Jesus showed consummate skill in demonstrating how his Father's truths struck a responsive chord in the minds of the people he lived and worked with.

The miracles of Jesus addressed daily concerns first and the power of God second. His very first miracle was not the establishment of the Holy Eucharist or walking on the sea. It was the changing of water into wine at Cana—a message, among others, that he endorsed and respected the miracle of human love.

He knew, too, that in the arid, harsh land where his listeners lived, without the benefit of the physicians and advanced medicaments of the twentieth century, personal health was an overriding concern, and so he performed many miracles to cure illnesses and even restore life. Almost one-third of the Gospel of St. Mark is devoted to chronicling the healing miracles. St. Luke records that the only specific directive Jesus gave to the seventy-two disciples when he sent them out to evangelize was "Cure the sick." And when he sent the twelve on a similar mission, he asked them to "proclaim the kingdom of God, and heal." He cured the psyche as well as the body. He wrote mysterious words in the sand that brought back a sense of self-respect to a woman who had been publicly shamed.

The parables reveal a corresponding recognition of personal needs. Jesus talked about illness, about finances, about how the Father cares for us more than for the sparrow. If Jesus were teaching today, he would send disciples out to heal those who have contacted AIDS. When he talked about finances, he would focus on the business people for whom the bottom line has become an obsession. He would use the examples of the Good Samaritan and the man who had to be carried into the pool of Siloam to speak to the victims of Alzheimer's disease and cancer. When he used the example of the sparrow to indicate the Father's love for each individual, he would remind us of the needs of the abused child. He would instruct the clothes-conscious teenager when describing the lilies of the field.

Even the sacraments show how Jesus applied spiritual messages and signs to everyday life. The signs he used were a part of the daily experiences of his listeners: bread and wine and water and oil and words and touch.

If the homilist is to give a message that will have meaning to the greatest number in his congregation, he must get their attention. He does this by identifying one or more of their basic interests and needs, and then by showing how the Word of God, contained in the readings of the day, fulfills those interests and needs.

Interesting—But Unpleasant—Topics

Clerics sometimes object to the concept of making a homily interesting, saying that a homilist does not have the obligation of telling the people "what they want to hear." The objection is justifiable; homilies do not have that purpose. However, we should not confuse what is pleasant for the congregation with what is of interest to them. The subject of lawful authority will not be palatable to teenagers, but it is one that interests them. Sharing one's goods with the poor may not be an intriguing topic for the average husband or wife, but the satisfaction that flows from sharing is of interest to everyone. These are not subjects to discuss every weekend, but they cannot be avoided simply because they are unpleasant. If homilists do not deliver and interpret these messages as well as the more pleasant ones, who will do it? Jesus did not hold back when telling the rich young man to sell all and give to the poor, or when driving the money-changers out of the temple.

Abortion is a "tough topic" that priests often shy away from because of the simple fact that they have been criticized in the past for what some claim has been an overemphasis on sex from the pulpit. Most priests don't want people to say, "There he goes again." Yet of all times for a homilist to refrain from touching on abortion, the 1990s is the least acceptable. It is, of course, a topic that must be approached with caution and good sense. A diatribe from the pulpit against "those who are murdering our children by the millions" will not be effective. Truth is truth, but it must be tempered with compassion and understanding.

Credible Messages

To win the attention of the congregation, then, the homilist must have a message that deals with the basic interests of a large proportion of the congregation. Second, he must present a message that is intellectually acceptable. It must be credible, that is, it must be a message that conforms with the way individual members of the congregation view their world. The homilist who speaks over the heads of the people or promises things that cannot be delivered is not believable.

Father Art, known for his education, his superb voice, and excellent delivery began a lenten homily with these words: "Today I would like to talk to you about the false philosophies we find all about us. What do I mean by a false philosophy? By false philosophy I mean the pragmatic concept of a materialistic world...." His audience was awakened only by the clinking of coins as the collection basket was passed around. Jay Cormier in *Giving Good Homilies* writes of another pastor who began his homily, addressed to a group of laborers, with these words: "My dear friends, in even the most cursory exegesis of this morning's gospel. . . ."

Both homilists failed to deliver a credible message simply because they were talking above the knowledge and background of the average congregation.

Other messages lack believability when they make guarantees that obviously cannot always be fulfilled. The promise of receiving a hundred-fold in return for tithing, the assurance that all prayers will be answered, the pledge that life will always improve through the study of Scripture must be used with caution. We do not suggest that you never include these kinds of assurances in a homily, but that when you do so, you should restrict yourself to the use of the subjunctive.

— 5 —

Know Where You Are Going

The homily should have a recognizable goal and objective

The preceding chapter outlined the first fundamental of successful communication: The message must in some way be of interest to the congregation. The second fundamental, if properly applied, is one step toward insuring that the congregation *will* be interested in what is being presented. The homilist should identify the goal and the specific objective of his presentation so that he knows where he is going and the assembly will be able to follow.

Goals of a Homily

Dictionaries define goal as an aim or a purpose. The goal answers the question, "Why am I delivering this message?" Goals are statements about the general purpose of a homily. They are usually qualitative in nature, reflecting broad aims for desired levels of accomplishment. Some of the goals for a homily may be to motivate, praise, criticize, warn, comfort, entertain, call for tolerance, persuade, inspire, eulogize, alert, caution, and offer hope.

Identifying a goal in the preparation of a homily is an important step for several reasons. First, a goal gives direction to the homily and sets a course for the congregation to follow. Trying to handle a canoe in a strong wind is difficult because the craft has no keel. Trying to deliver a homily without a goal is equally difficult.

Congregation members will quickly be able to determine whether the homily has a goal. If it has, they are likely to respond with attention. If it doesn't, they will turn off their hearing aids and wait grimly, usually with admirable Christian patience, for the ceremony to continue.

Second, a goal will prevent the inclusion of non-essentials.

FF: I once reviewed a homily with my friend George Freund and asked if the addition of a very interesting story would make the homily too long. George replied, "I'm not concerned about the length. Does the story have anything to do with the reason [goal] you are giving the homily?" The story was not pertinent, but, still, it was difficult to omit it. George correctly advised deleting the story.

Every side issue that leads the attention of the congregation away from the goal of the message can only detract from the effectiveness of the homily.

Third, the homilist who has not specified the goal can easily find himself going in the same direction Sunday after Sunday. If on every occasion he educates, criticizes, or inspires, the congregation will soon turn him off. Messages that are predictable become tiresome, even homilies.

FF: I remember the invariability of the meals in the seminary. Meat loaf of Monday, pork chops on Tuesday, chicken on Wednesday. The meals were good, but just too predictable. When I was invited out to dinner, the invitation was accepted readily not because I was assured of a better meal, but because I wanted a change.

Fourth, varying the goal increases the number of potential homilies that can be prepared. Using the same readings, the homilist can change the goal and have several different presentations. Currently the Sunday readings are repeated in three-year cycles. The homilist who alters the goal relative to those readings will continually be able to bring new insights to the congregation and a welcome freshness to his Sunday messages.

The human mind has three functions: the intellectual, the affective or emotional, and the volitional. Each goal of a homily will appeal to one or more of these mental functions. Education is directed toward the intellectual, promoting understanding; praise and affirmation, to the affective, bringing satisfaction; motivation and inspiration, to the volitional, leading to decisions and actions. When a homilist does not establish goals, the majority of his homilies tend to become educational. Congregations need more than education. The art of communication is like a three-legged stool. For the minds of the congregation to be continually stimulated, and to keep the efforts of the homilist in balance, all three types of homily, all three legs, are needed.

Specific Objective of a Homily

In addition to having a goal, each homily should have at least one specific objective. Goals serve as guidelines for objectives. Objectives are more specific, often quantifiable aims that are achievable at a definite point in time.

If the goal of the homilist is to motivate, the question arises, "Motivate to do what?" Perhaps to contribute more generously to the parish, help with the youth group, coach a basketball team, or become involved in a Bible study group. He might encourage them to attend daily Mass, visit the sick, speak out against racism, spend more time with their children, become active in the fight against abortion, or attend the upcoming Mission.

Identifying an objective is only the starting point in its achievement. Nothing will be accomplished unless even more precise suggestions are made. The homilist outlines for the congregation how, when, and where the parishioners should carry out the objective. Goals reflect broad aims, but objectives are specific. For this reason, the homilist must provide the congregation with specific tools and directions to accomplish the objective.

We find the application of these principles in the parables of Jesus. Is there a better example of *education* than Christ's sermon on the Mount? Matthew writes, "He began to teach them." Education was the goal but the specific objective was to teach truths that went beyond the scope of Jewish laws. He asked for very specific conduct: Be merciful, meek, and clean of heart. He didn't stop there; he indicated how these actions would *benefit* his listeners. They would receive mercy, inherit the land, see God.

Christ often tried to *inspire*. A man asked him, "What must I do to inherit eternal life?" Christ first tried to motivate him, but when that did not satisfy the man, Jesus asked him to take a quantum leap of faith. He tried to *inspire* him, asking him to take a specific action. "Sell everything you have." Why? "So that you will have treasure in heaven." *When?* "Now, come follow me." Christ asked for a complete change in the man's lifestyle.

As the homilist completes this exercise for each homily, he will have determined a goal that will give a direction to the presentation. As he specifies the objective, he defines the scope of the goal, narrows the focus of the message, and guides the congregation through the steps that must be taken for goal to be accomplished.

EM: My goal in sports was not to be enshrined in the Basketball Hall of Fame. As an awkward 13 year old, that would have been very presumptuous. My goals pertained to my practice sessions. One goal was to become a great shooter. My specific objectives were to develop a jump shot, a lay up, and a hook shot. My plan of action included a practice schedule, watching great players, and playing against better competition. Another goal was to become a great scorer, which is much different than becoming a good shooter. The objectives leading to becoming a scorer were to learn to play one-on-one to beat the defensive man; to learn to use other players to set screens in order to get open; to develop speed, running the court to beat other men to the basket; to practice under pressure so that game-winning baskets resulted. I had other goals, such as becoming a fine rebounder, passer, and defensive player. The result was membership in the Basketball Hall of Fame.

The same is true of homilies. Now I set a goal, identify specific objectives, and suggest a plan of action for every homily. I can tell if I reach the goal by the comments of the congregation following the service. If there are no comments, pro or con, I probably haven't reached my goal.

Tips on Using Goals

1. *Stick with the goal.* When praising the audience, do so and leave out the "buts." (You're doing a fine job, but. . .) Tell the parishioners they've done a fine job and leave it at that. If you have further comments regarding their deficiencies, leave those for a later homily.

2. *Vary the goal.* To avoid repetition, develop a long-range plan. Draw up a list of goals for the next 6 Sunday homilies. Notice how easy it is to slip into the practice of having the same goal every Sunday. Change the goal and you will bring life and variety to the message.

St. Paul varied the goal of his messages frequently. In Romans 1, he praises his readers by telling them their faith is known the world over. In verse 20 he criticizes. In 5:1 he consoles and in 6:12 he exhorts them. (St. Paul did not act against our suggestion about using only one goal in the same message. He was not giving counsel to the Romans Sunday after Sunday. Rather, his communications were often separated by years. He could not afford the luxury of waiting until the next letter for his admonitions.) His letters to the Corinthians are full of counsel and motivation. His letter to the Philippians is an example of praise and love and encouragement.

Since education plays a significant part in the background of most homilists, the temptation comes easily to cast every message in a teaching mode. Although that would be a mistake, education *is* a legitimate goal for a homily. The skillful homilist can make use of a teaching message on occasion, if he has prepared the homily in such a way that the congregation will have the "ah-ha" experience, that sudden insight or realization that one has "discovered" something. An effective instructional homily not only educates, but it awakens insights into the meaning of Scripture and an awareness of how our lives may be contrary to the implications found there.

After one priest washed the feet of twelve congregation members at the Holy Thursday liturgy, he described the way Jesus explained this gesture to the perplexed apostles. Precisely because he was Lord and master, it was necessary for Jesus to perform that act of service. In this way, the homilist implied how parents should act toward their children, and how employers should treat their employees. The congregation got the message. They were not told how to treat their employees, their families, or the recluse down the block, but many of them must have gone home with an insight into human relationships that was clearer and more compelling than what would have resulted from a strong, direct exhortation.

Education that leads to the ah-ha experience can be a very effective way to increase the faith of parishioners in the reality of God, in God's love and concern for us, and in what lies in store for us after judgment.

The search for and identification of goals and specific objectives for each homily can be as challenging as a crossword puzzle. What do the parishioners need at this point in the history of the parish? Are they ready for motivation, praise, encouragement, sympathy, education? The homilist must study the parish thoroughly in order to determine the congregation's needs. He should listen to the conversations of the people, note what is being said in coffee klatches, observe the problems of the neighborhood, and be aware of the trends of society. Designing homilies to fit these needs brings an excitement to the process of preparing each message.

We were discussing this question of the needs of a parish with a gentleman whose answer was as perceptive as any we have heard. "The homilist should walk into the pulpit with a Bible in one hand and the daily newspaper in the other." He touched on one of the principal secrets of delivering effective homilies. The daily paper reflects the lives of the people. It reflects their problems, their hopes, their fears. The Bible, the Word of God, provides the guidance they need to live their lives according to God's wonderful plan.

— 6 —

Avoid Side Trips

The homily should have a single topic

Some homilists use multiple topics in the hope that the congregation will remember and respond to at least one of them. The practice is self-defeating. The first and most obvious reason is that most audiences can absorb only one topic at a time.

A second reason for avoiding multiple topics is that the total number of significant messages geared to the needs of a particular congregation has limits. The average homilist must deliver sixty to sixty-five addresses each year to the same audience. His assignment to a parish might be for a period of ten or twelve years. Because he must speak frequently to the same group, it is vital for him to avoid choosing topics recklessly. Making use of several topics on each occasion rapidly diminishes the number of topics available. Rev. Henry Dohlman had been at Saint Marie's parish for thirty-five years. One day he asked the bishop to be transferred, because he had finally run out of ideas for his Sunday homilies. The bishop replied, "Henry, your parishioners tell me you ran out of ideas years ago." Carefully selecting one topic per homily will avoid the doldrums of re-runs.

Finally, using one topic in a homily presents advantages to the homilist. Identifying a topic, staying with it, and bringing the homily to a logical conclusion diminishes the preparation time and increases the effectiveness of the homilist. Everyone benefits.

Clyde Fant in *Preaching for Today* advises us: "A three-point sermon, each with three sub-points is a nine-point [topic] sermon. All a preacher can do with a sermon like that is talk himself to death trying to explain so many ideas."

Some refer to the multiple-topic approach as a "laundry list." The most common violator of the principle of a single topic is the homilist who is convinced that liturgically he has not satisfied his obligation unless he has, on every occasion, explained all three readings, plus the responsorial psalm. There is a painful dullness in the homily in which the preacher tells his audience that the first reading means this, the second reading means that, and the third means something else. Such a homily involves exegesis, not preaching, and exegesis, except on a very limited scale, belongs in the preparation of the homily, not in its presentation.

While the scriptural readings are carefully selected and combined because of a common element—a theme or motif found in each—the extraction of every relationship that exists among the readings is more the province of the Scripture scholar than of the homilist. Even when the theme is clearly interwoven in all of the readings, it is more effective for the homilist, and more understandable to the congregation, to select one of the readings as the primary source of reflection, and to briefly bring in the other readings.

Defining the Topic

How does the homilist determine the topic for his presentation? The term "topic" does not refer to the Scripture reading or a portion of it that has been selected as the basis for the homily. Nor does it refer to the general goal of the homily, such as urging, praising, or warning. Nor is the topic the same as the specific objective of the homily, such as encouraging the members of the audience to make appropriate use of their gifts: talents, skills, money, power, time, health. A topic is a *message* that the homilist wishes to give to the congregation. It is the subject of his treatise and the fruit of his reflection and prayer.

The homilist need not rack his brains, seeking hidden, unique meanings buried within the readings. In fact, all too often such insights are abstract theological concepts, excellent for understanding the readings and for preparing a message, but hardly the stuff of which homilies are made. A significant and meaningful topic will come to the homilist after he has reflected on two things: 1) the readings themselves, and 2) how those readings speak to the lives and problems, the interests and concerns of the people. Each week the homilist needs to answer this question: What is there in the daily experiences of my congregation, what is there about important events now happening in this community, in the nation, and in the world, for which today's readings are pertinent?

When determining a topic, the homilist might heed the advice from the previous chapter: Take a Bible and a daily newspaper into the pulpit. If the *New York Times* were published in the time of Christ, he would likely have gotten topics for his parables from its pages. Perhaps he would have started a parable like this:

> Many of you have seen the story in this morning's Times regarding the man who decided to settle accounts with his servant. The kingdom of heaven is like that story. Let me explain. The kingdom of heaven is also like the story on yesterday's financial page, the story of three men and their talents. It is like the news story of the workers in the vineyard. It is like the report on the society page about the man who held a wedding feast and no one came.

The fact that these stories are still told 2000 years later attests to their effectiveness. The same technique is available to every homilist.

Events that were current in the summer of 1992 were the summer Olympics, the political races, scandals in Washington, D.C., bias in the media, and the riots in Los Angeles. A sad commentary appeared during this time in the letters to the editor of the archdiocesan newspaper in St. Louis, stating that homilists on the Sunday following the Los Angeles tragedy did not even mention the death and destruction in that city.

Sometimes the homilist will say, "I just don't know what to speak about this Sunday." If the homilist reflects on the readings and how they concern the lives of the people, as suggested above, there will be so much to say that the only difficulty will be how to limit one's remarks within the time frame of a Sunday homily.

The topic, the message, is a one-line summary of the entire homily. Herein lies a simple criterion by which to judge whether or not the homily has a single topic. If it can be summarized in a single sentence, it has only one topic; if more than one sentence is needed, there probably is more than one topic.

Avoiding a multiplicity of topics does not mean that there cannot be sub-points in the message, or that side issues cannot be introduced. Both additions can give structure, foundation, and color to a homily. But only *one* principal issue should be addressed. Too many side trips will only confuse the congregation. On a trip from New York to Chicago, there is nothing wrong with stopping a few days in Philadelphia or taking a side trip to some historic location. However, remember where you are going. Side trips involve diversions and delays. The goal is still Chicago, not Philadelphia, Columbus, Toronto, or Detroit.

Often so many possible topics are found in a single reading that the homilist must carefully study and select the one most appropriate to use on this particular occasion. The choice will be determined sometimes by the liturgical season; at other times by the special needs of this congregation, needs that vary with the current events affecting the community and the parish—war and peace, prosperity and poverty, achievements and failures, joys and sorrows, a recent accident, an incident of dishonesty, a government decision, the six rows of empty pews after communion that cause the speaker to wonder about the belief of the congregation in the reality of the Eucharist.

Interest Factor

The homilist may be further guided in his selection of a topic by the inclusion of an interest factor. We pointed out in an earlier chapter that unless the topic selected is of interest to the audience they will not listen. Often the process of choosing and precisely defining a topic is made easier by selecting an interest factor and developing the homily around it. By an interest factor, we mean a specific need or concern, present in this congregation, at this Mass, which will make the selected topic meaningful to the audience.

The writers have discovered in discussions with parishioners that there are many topics of vital interest that are rarely discussed in the pulpit. Here are some observations they have made:

My son attends a public high school in which evolution is taught with a denial that God created the world. I have never heard a word from the pulpit about this subject, and there are three high schools in the district, all teaching the same concept. Won't someone help us?

Fifty percent of all marriages end in divorce today. I have a daughter who is divorced. My grandchildren are torn between the two parents. I never have heard a homily on the sadness that comes from divorce.

In 1991, we learned that the basketball star, Magic Johnson, contracted the HIV virus. I have never heard a word from the pulpit about the number of young women he may have infected. Does anyone have an opinion about how the world selects its heroes? I wish someone would say something about this topic.

Our government tried to pass a balanced budget. They couldn't do it. Our children will pay a fearful price because we waste so much money. Jesus asked us to be good stewards.

There was a school board election, and most of the candidates favored giving out condoms at the high school. One opposed it. We hear nothing from the pulpit about how distributing condoms exposes our children to devastating disease. Why not?

If he listens well, every homilist will hear such comments from his parishioners. There is no lack of interest among them regarding these and other crucial problems of our day.

The Prodigal Son
Let us review some of the terms we have discussed in this and in

previous chapters, and their application to the preparation of a homily: goal, objective, topic, and interest factor. To exemplify the use of these terms, consider the parable of the Prodigal Son (Lk. 15:11–32). What are some possible goals, objectives, topics, and interest factors that might be used once you have selected a specific portion of the gospel text on which to build a homily?

1. *Portion of reading used.* One son asks his father for something he is not yet entitled to, his inheritance.

Goal. Warning.

Objective. To make the commandments come alive by showing their application to our daily lives.

Topic (message). The commandments tell us that only when we use our inheritance (gifts, talents, time) properly and at the opportune moment will we be blessed with peace and satisfaction.

Interest factor. Happiness. Everyone wants to be happy. Happiness does not result from making decisions contrary to the commandments.

2. *Portion of reading used.* Christ did not criticize the father for having been generous with his son.

Goal. Consolation.

Objective. To comfort parents who often feel they are completely responsible for the actions of their children. To let them know that all they can do is their best.

Topic. The actions of the son brought heartbreak to the parents; yet had they been guilty of malfeasance, Jesus would have said so in his story. (Notice where he places the blame: squarely on the shoulders of the offspring.)

Interest factor. The consolation needed by parents. All parents today are conscious of having only limited control over the lives of their children. Parents can do everything right, yet at some point in their lives, the decisions to be made and the consequences of those decisions rest with the children. A single experience with cocaine can doom their child.

3. *Portion of the reading used.* The son squandered his money on dissolute living.

Goal. Warning.

Objective. To get the members of the congregation to put themselves in the place of the prodigal son.

Topic. Are not the sins we commit very similar to those of the younger son, and are we, then, not squandering God's blessings, our inheritance?

Interest factor. Individuals in the audience realize the losses they can experience through the waste of opportunities in their personal or business life. The losses from wasted opportunities in our spiritual life are far greater.

4. *Portion of the reading used.* The son lost everything. He was broke and had to work with the swine. He had little food and no friends. He had hit bottom.

Goal. Hope.

Objective. To get people to trust that God offers hope in the most hopeless situations.

Topic. When one is seventeen and pregnant, when one is an alcoholic and alone, someone is always there for us, one person is always waiting to receive us and forgive.

Interest factor. No one wants to be alone. No situation is hopeless. Other people usually help; God always does. Hope is the interest factor.

5. *Portion of the reading used.* Then he made a decision: He would go home. That decision changed his life. Eventually his father gave him more than he could have imagined.

Goal. Inspiration.

Objective. To remind people of the incredible mercy, forgiveness, and generosity of God, the Father, and lead them to make decisions that reflect their belief in these qualities.

Topic. No matter what kind of life we have lived, we must become aware of the kindness of the Father. Jesus tried to impress this fact on us when he told us that the father in the parable was in fact his Father, and ours.

Interest factor. Everyone wants a second chance. With the Father there is an endless series of second chances offered right up to the final moment of our lives.

6. *Portion of the reading used.* After making the decision, he set out for home. Did you ever wonder how he got home? It must have been a difficult trip; it was certainly not first class on United Airlines. But he did make the trip, and the reward was worthwhile.

Goal. Motivation.

Objective. To show people the value of making a difficult decision.

Topic. The simplest changes in our lives are often the most difficult. Because the trip is hard, we shy away from visiting the sick, forgiving someone after an argument, reconciling ourselves with an antagonist.

Interest factor. The recognized need of people to overcome inertia and act. Action itself leads to solutions, and God will help. God will provide the fish, but we must dig for the bait.

When preparing a homily, the order of determining each element is not necessarily as we just listed them. The starting point could be the goal, the objective, the topic, or the interest factor. The order of the elements is selected after the homilist has reflected on the meanings of the day's readings.

Let's see how it works. If war were declared during the week, it would seem logical that the preacher would select that conflict as the topic of the Sunday homily. As the preparation progresses, however, any number of goals could come to mind. Would the homilist choose to motivate the congregation, inspire them, or warn them? The objective would depend upon the goal: Would he motivate them to pray, inspire them to come together as a nation and as families and to discharge their duty to their country? Would he warn them of the difficult times ahead? The interest factor would be simple. In times of stress, everyone seeks reassurance.

In another situation, the objective might be the starting point. The parish may be in debt, and the objective could be "increasing the amount donated to the church." Once this objective is chosen, a goal needs to be selected. Do you wish to motivate the parishioners to give more money, educate them, or inspire them to sacrificial giving?

Note how changing the goal of a homily will alter the remaining components, and could become the basis for a number of homilies. Suppose we change the goal of the first example above on the parable of the Prodigal Son, "warning," to "promoting the concept of stewardship." An appropriate objective then might be to show what happens when we misuse our inheritance, the gifts and talents God has given us. The topic might be something like this: The son wound up in a pig sty, and the same thing can happen to us. The interest factor: No one wants to lose health, family, and friends.

Even more flexibility in the choice of topics is present when the concepts found in a portion of the reading are applied to specific age groups in the audience, as described in Chapter 4, on interest. The homogeneity of a particular congregation, such as is found in the children's school day liturgy, presents a special opportunity to make the homily meaningful. When the audience is mixed, as it is on weekends, an awareness of the various age groups present will enable the homilist to enrich his message by making applications to each group, and thus to fulfill fundamentals 1 (The homily should be of interest to the congregation) and 5 (The homily should address everyone in the congregation).

The topics we have listed are not deeply theological, nor were they intended to be. They are practical topics, the kind Christ discussed when he was preaching. The concerns of the ordinary congregation are not deeply theological. Parishioners come to the liturgy with very ordinary problems that are immediate, simple, pressing, and most frequently, familial. If we wish people to relate to the homily, these are the topics that need to be addressed. When a homilist deals only with issues that occupy the time of the professor in courses of religious studies, people soon come to the conclusion, rightly or wrongly, that the Liturgy of the Word really doesn't matter, that it is not relevant to their daily lives, perhaps even that Christ was not genuinely concerned about their daily problems.

FF: Father Nick Lentz, a close friend of mine who died in 1950, was one of the most beloved priests of the Archdiocese of Dubuque. He once took me aside and gave me some wise counsel about preaching. "The people who come to Mass on Sunday have had, more often than not, all kinds of minor tragedies in their lives. Johnny broke a window in the church basement; Janie got poor marks on her report card; the special meal mother planned for company did not turn out well; Dad is faced with the possible termination of his job; the family might have to move to a new town, or cut down on their standard of living." And he continued, "Often they face a diatribe from the pastor; he scolds them for their lack of virtue or for their failure to contribute to the building fund. I know how they are hurting inside, even when they greet me with a warm good morning, and so I spend much of my homily time telling them how good they are, how much God loves them, and how kind and forgiving God is. Then, once a year, just to let them know that I am really not a dummy, I prepare a homily on one of the most difficult topics I can think of, full of theological disputation and erudite expressions, but only once a year."

Father Lentz might not rank high as a theologian, but his parishioners loved him. They saw in him a reflection of Jesus, and they learned more about the divine characteristics from him than they could have learned from a high-level classroom instruction. When he was dying as the result of a severe stroke, the parishioners turned out in great numbers and prayed for him in the church all through the night. He knew their concerns and their needs as well as any homilist I have ever known.

Looking only at the broad meaning of a reading limits the potential number of messages. The lives of the congregation are immersed in specific circumstances, problems, and opportunities; they do not live in broad, general situations. By concentrating on individual segments of a reading the homilist can find any number of applications for the audience.

We have mentioned that simply changing the goal of a homily

can alter the remaining elements: objective, topic, and interest factor. Similarly, changing the objective can modify the homily. For example, the objective for each of the six topics suggested for the parable of the Prodigal Son could be changed to provide the basis for three or four homilies; thus at a minimum there are fifteen to twenty potential homilies in the five topics listed. These topics relate to the audience, not to classroom theology. They are not lectures, but simple messages addressed to the everyday concerns of the congregation. Within every congregation there *are* innumerable problems and difficulties faced daily and thus an almost unlimited number of potential topics for the homilist.

—7—

Spell It Out

The homily should be specific

==

The fourth fundamental of good homiletic communication is concerned with specificity. A congregation cannot easily understand a message that is general.

Madison Avenue advertising has been the subject of frequent polemics because of its obvious materialism. Yet the corporations that make use of this type of advertising are not noted for spending huge amounts of money just to keep the advertising companies in business. The techniques may be objectionable, but they are effective. Testimony to that fact will be given by any mother who writes a check for $150 for Sam's athletic shoes or Mary's designer jeans—by any father who is constrained to buy every piece of Nintendo equipment. Madison Avenue advertising is effective for several reasons. It uses proven market research tools to identify the needs of the public; it is colorful, imaginative, and often humorous. But primarily it is specific. Radio and television commercials do not direct your attention to a group of products, but to a single item that will, they imply, solve all your problems, make you the most attractive individual in the world, and bring you instant success. The ads leave you in no doubt about what the benefits of using their product will be. This type of advertising does not promote reality, but it is extraordinarily successful communication, ev~ the most sophisticated audience.

Those who wish to be successful in oral communication need to employ a comparable technique. Specificity in a message has a powerful attraction for both viewers and listeners. The more general the message of the homilist, the less effective will that message be for the average congregation.

> FF: Whenever this subject comes up, I recall the remark of my close friend, Clarence Friedman, who could not put up with a general invitation. He wanted invitations to be spelled out; what day should I come, and at what time? Priest confreres or members of the parish would say to him, "Come to see me sometime." Father Friedman's blunt reply would be, "Sometime means never."

There are two ways in which the homilist should be specific: 1) in the terms used, and 2) in the examples given.

Using Specific Terms
If the homilist uses nebulous and universal terms, the congregation can hide behind the general nature of the message and never realize that it is directed to them personally. The homily should be so constructed that each individual in the congregation has the impression that he or she is the only one in the church being addressed.

Adolph Hitler is sitting in the audience, and the message is, "Love your neighbor." If the message remains at this level of generality, the homily will probably have no effect on him. He could answer, "You are absolutely correct. That is why I am so happy that I have been able to help my German people. See what I have done to assist Czechoslovakia; now I am marching into Russia and will save Christianity by ending the Communist rule there." I might shake my head and protest, "That's not what I meant!" It was not, of course, but my remarks were so general that Hitler could make his own decision on how the admonition should be interpreted.

If the homilist said, "Your neighbors are the Jews. Your neighbors are the priests and ministers you are arresting and putting in concentration camps, and you, Adolph Hitler, are violating the commandment to love your neighbor," Adolph would have a different reaction. One of them, of course, might be to invite you into one of his camps, but at least there would be no doubt in his mind regarding the thrust of your message.

The use of general statements in a homily accomplishes little. Telling an audience to "Love thy neighbor" is so universal that it has no meaning. It is like Father Friedman's "Come to visit me sometime." All people judge that they love their neighbor in some ways.

"Develop your faith" is an admonition that will cause the congregation to nod their heads and do nothing. "Develop a personal relationship with Jesus by praying directly to him each morning before you leave the house, each evening as you turn off the TV" is more likely to add to the prayer life of members of the congregation. The homily that remains on the level of general statements allows the audience to concentrate on its virtues and ignore its faults. When someone tells me to love my neighbor, I mentally recall all the good things I do for my neighbor. I justify my behavior and congratulate myself on having fulfilled the commandment. But if a homilist were specific and defined as my neighbor a poor family whose name and needs I know, my reaction would be different. If I am asked, "How much time did you spend working at the food pantry for the homeless this past week, or visiting someone in a hospital, or calling on an elderly friend?" I am prompted to reflect on what positive contributions I have made the past week to my neighbor's welfare. When I make that reflection, I will come up with specific answers to the questions, one of which might be that I did very little.

For adults, a general term is "your neighbor"; more specific is "the fellow on your block who can't pay his rent," or "the newcomer in the neighborhood," or "someone on your street who is sick or lonely," or "someone who has AIDS." "Society" is a general term; "the members of your country club" is specific. "Fellow workers" is general; "the secretary in your office" is specific. "The poor" is general; "the parish list of those needing Christmas baskets" is specific.

For adolescents, a general term is "your neighbor"; specific terms are "your mother who is a good listener and who cooks for you," "your father who watches your baseball games and pays for your tuition." "Bad habits" is a general term; specific terms are "using drugs," "premarital sex," "cheating on your exams," "taking advantage of your customers or employer." "The evils of society" is a general term; "racism"and "sexism" are specific. "Serving your community" is a general term; "running for office," "voting," and "writing letters to the editor" are specific.

Some homilists hide behind general terms because the use of specific terminology can be embarrassing for them and provocative for the congregation. By avoiding specifics, they elude stirring up a hornet's nest. They are also bland, soporific, and ineffectual.

Using Specific Examples

Christ did not deal in generalities; he used specific examples. He constantly referred to situations familiar to everyone: the farmer who went out to sow his field; the shepherd who risked his life for his sheep; the woman who lost the coin and swept the house searching for it; the man who found a buried treasure in his field; the owner of the vineyard who came to the village square looking for workers; the worker in the vineyard who was paid the same wage for working fewer hours than others did. Every parable and every story was based on an individual or a situation well known to his listeners. The lesson of the parables was not always evident, but the actions and the players of those little dramas were a familiar part of the pastoral setting of the people.

The homilist may comment, "But the average audience doesn't want to hear such mundane messages. They want more profound, philosophical discourses, more messages expounding the precise theological meaning of Christ's words." Not true. The average audience is not prepared to deal with that level of discourse in a Sunday homily. They are battling each week to keep their jobs, their spouses, the respect and love of their children, and their sanity. They want someone to help them with the problems they face today, tomorrow, and on Wednesday. They live with the temptation, though married, to date their secretaries, to keep everything they have for themselves and not to share, to avoid prayer, to satisfy their own needs without caring for their neighbor. They have read newspapers and magazines that deny creation, limit heaven and hell to our present state of existence, portray Christ as a wandering misfit, and ridicule the dogma of the virgin birth—and they need to be sustained in their faith. One of the reasons they come to the Sunday liturgy, even weekday liturgies, is to learn the Christian approach and answers to their problems. What does revelation have to say about my life? About Joe and Mary's marriage, about the growing pains of Ed, Sam and Joanne's son? Christ's messages offered hope to his followers, if only they were willing to change their lives as he requested. They followed him in droves.

Recently Father Cutlass gave a homily using specific examples. The readings of the day included Christ's reference to cutting off one's hand and plucking out one's eye if they should be the cause of scandal. Father asked what things Christ would identify as scandals if he were speaking today. He suggested that Christ would speak of the social sins of discrimination, sexual harassment, and taking advantage of the plight of migratory workers, and perhaps also of the use of pornographic videocassettes obtained at the video rental outlet. He said that Christ might advise you to think about cutting off your hand when you write a check for substandard wages for a migratory worker, or plucking out your eye when you view an off-color video. The counsel was hyperbolic, but naming specific instances that occupy the thoughts and sometimes the actions of congregation members gave them much to think about. Some will say this is "tough talk." Of course it is. But only a casual reading of the gospels will reveal that this homily did not even approach the toughness of some of the messages Christ delivered to his audiences. "Whitened sepulchers" is hardly a caressing address.

Being specific does not necessarily mean being critical. It is equally important to be specific when being positive. When praising the congregation, for example, it is important to specify who are being praised: the coaches who work with the grade school soccer team, the men and women who manage the parish fair, the teenagers who do volunteer work in the nursing home, the mothers and fathers who make sure their children attend Sunday Mass, the pro-life group, and others.

FF: An aside here. We mentioned that people come even to weekday liturgies in the hope of receiving insights that will better their lives. Although Vatican Council II definitely encouraged the practice of the weekday homily, I chose for some time to give no more than the weekend homily, excusing myself with what I thought was a humorous but practical rebuttal: "I find it difficult enough to be brilliant on Sunday, without trying to achieve that goal seven days a week." Then I was appointed to a large parish where it was an established practice to give a daily homily. Not wishing to make an immediate change in parish policy, I followed suit. I soon found it was not necessary to be brilliant, or even bright, for the weekday homily. The comments from people were both rewarding and enlightening. They did not say they had learned new elements of theology during the week, or that they now better understood the mystery of the Holy Spirit. They said that whatever came through by way of these reflections on the daily readings gave them strength for the day, courage and energy to face their problems, and a better understanding of what it meant to be a Christian.

Sophistication is neither required nor particularly helpful in a homily. That is why we say, "Keep it simple." Spell it out. The Curé of Ars was one of the simplest, and one of the most effective preachers of all time. Don't beat around the bush. Tell the people what Christ or what God is saying and how it refers to their lives today, tomorrow, next week, and next month. Generalities are mush.

— 8 —

So What?

The homily should ask for specific action

In addition to using specific terms and examples, the homilist should often call for specific action, either something to be done or an attitude to be changed. Love your neighbor calls for a change of attitude; visit that neighbor in the hospital calls for something to be carried out.

The fundamental goal of *any* form of communication is to produce a noticeable effect upon an audience. The purpose of the discourses and parables of Jesus was to convert his hearers into disciples, to make them aware of the existence of the Reign of God and their opportunity and their obligation to serve that kingdom. Bishop Morneau writes: "Homilies are more than mere invitations. They contain an imperative that demands a response" ("A Preacher's Notebook—Personal Resource Center" in *Preaching Better*).

If a communicator presents a truth without letting the audience know how that truth speaks to their present situation, the message lacks relevance. It's like telling a joke but failing to deliver the punch line; like reading a book and finding the final chapter missing. It's like proposing a riddle and not giving the answer. Unless those in the audience are able to grasp that some kind of action, or at least a change in attitude is expected, they may understand the message, but will do nothing about it.

In the letter of St. James, in which the apostle advises charity toward the unfed and the ill-clad, the writer evidently faced a situation that did not call for subtle suggestion or offering opportunities. He needed to communicate a specific call to action, and he did not hesitate to do so.

> If a brother or sister has nothing to wear and has no food for the day, and one of you says to them, "Go in peace, keep warm, and eat well," but you do not give them the necessities of the body, what good is it? So also faith of itself, if it does not have good works, is dead (2:15–17).

A homily that purports to address itself to the relevant issues of the lives of the congregation but does not guide them into some kind of action may be described in the same way: dead. Christ seldom asked for general actions. He came to the point. "Give up everything and follow me." "Take up your bed and walk." "Go and do likewise." "Lazarus, come forth." "Begone, Satan." "Unless you become like children you will never enter the kingdom of heaven."

We do not recommend that a homilist get the reputation of being a "vegetable garden" speaker, one who ends every message with the all-too-familiar "therefore lettuce do this and lettuce do that." However, many homilies should conclude by encouraging specific actions from the congregation. The parish objectives have not been reached; the school has not been supported; the liturgy is languishing. Action is called for, and it is the obligation of the homilist to make the call. In such instances the homily needs to be specific not only with regard to terminology and examples (see Chapter 7), but also in the actions requested.

Christ found those occasions, too, and did not hesitate to be specific. "Come after me." "Whoever puts his hand to the plow but keeps looking back is unfit for the reign of God." "Take up your bed and walk." "Neither do I condemn you; go, and do not sin again." His parables, and very often the miracles, were followed by very specific requests for action. The homilist who asks for action will have communicated the full message of Christ to the audience—an invitation and a request for a response.

When the homilist makes such a request, what he asks must be transparently clear. Television and radio commercials avoid ambiguity in their calls to action. "Buy Irish Spring soap today." And if the product is to be purchased over the telephone there isn't the slightest doubt about what that phone number is. It is highlighted on the screen, and in case your eyes wander from the screen, it is repeated several times. "Call now, 1-800-555-3434; that's 1-800-555-3434." Amazingly, those ads are very successful. The homilist will do well to emulate their invitation for direct action. The Christian message advertises products much more attractive, far more fulfilling. Society has problems, Christianity has answers.

Examples

What are some specific actions that may be asked of children? "Say your morning and evening prayers." "Learn the acts of faith, hope, and contrition this week." "Tell your mother you love her." "Clean up your room." "Wash the dishes." "Thank your father for attending the play you were in, for driving you to day camp. To show your thanks, put the clean dishes away; help rake the leaves."

Some actions that may be suggested to parents: "Talk to your children; tell them you trust them; give them areas of responsibility. Above all, tell them you love them, again and again." "Turn to a rap station when driving with them. If the lyrics are offensive, discuss them with your child."

Actions for adults and youngsters together: "Help a poor family in your neighborhood not with money, but with household chores; take a meal to a family that has just moved into the neighborhood." "Work during elections; pick a candidate and work for her or him." For married couples: "When did you last say to your spouse, 'I love you'?"

How do you make specific the request to read the Bible more? Father McKay handles this task very well. After the homily, he tells the congregation which readings he thought were particularly beautiful or especially poetic or suitable for meditation. Then he says, "When we sit down for reflection just before the final prayer, pick up your missalette and go over that reading slowly and carefully, and see how some particular verse in that reading can make you a better person if you really put it into practice." Of all the hundreds of pastors and associates whose Masses we have attended, this priest was one of the few in our memory who spelled out in exact terms what he wanted the congregation to do during the meditation period following the Eucharistic Prayer. In all probability, that congregation was one of the few who realized what they were doing during the period of reflection. (Did we hear someone say that the missalette is obsolete?)

> EM: I finished one of my homilies by suggesting that the congregation read the letter of James, sent to the Jews living in Rome and Greece, whose societies were much like our own. After the Mass, one couple remarked jokingly, "Are you going to start giving us homework?" The husband said, "You've convinced us; we are going to read that letter." Then with a puzzled look on his face, he turned to his wife and asked, "By the way, where is our Bible?" I don't know if they read the letter, but I do know they heard my request for action.

Some areas where action is to be recommended are very sensitive. How does the homilist go about handling, delicately but effectively, the following situations?

Telling well-to-do congregations they must share more of their material wealth with others less fortunate.

Admonishing a group of business executives that the teaching of Christ to pay employees a just wage means that employees must be compensated enough to enable them to enjoy a decent standard of living.

Instructing union members that it is dishonest not to work a full day for a full day's pay.

Telling the congregation that premarital sex is immoral, even when you are in love.

1. *Point out opportunities.* Instead of directly making an appeal for action, the homilist might simply suggest opportunities for

Christian activity that are implied in the readings of the day. If the readings recommend prayer or the study of Scripture, the homilist could suggest that individuals have time to say the rosary when driving their car to and from work, the supermarket, or college. He might suggest that a reading of the Scriptures before leaving for work or school would give a person the opportunity to do some reflective meditation during a time that is normally non-productive. (Watching the traffic lights is not a full-time job for the active mind; important, of course, but not an all-consuming exercise.) More heroic activities might be encouraged, but if we can't follow Christ's admonitions in small things we do every day, we can't hope to achieve success in the more advanced applications of Christianity. By offering such suggestions, the preacher is not telling the people what to do. He is pointing out opportunities for Christian practices that are present in the life of every person.

2. *Ask questions*. A second way of achieving closure in a homily, short of asking for specific action, is to ask what Christ would do in various situations, or how he would apply the lessons to people today. Would the Good Shepherd be someone who would not drink and then drive? Would the Good Samaritan be the father who spends time with each of his children to try to understand what is going on in their lives? With every set of readings there are questions to be raised that apply to a contemporary audience. The effectiveness of this approach is that the *hearer* draws the appropriate conclusions and makes the applications that are only subtly suggested by the questions proposed by the homilist. Drawing your own conclusions involves the ego and helps form a commitment. Forming your own conclusions causes you to buy into a project, a decision, a change in attitude.

3. *Bide your time*. The standard advice given to a new pastor is "Don't begin your tenure by making changes." It is important for the homilist to first build a good relationship with the members of his parish. Only after that relationship is established can he successfully make requests for action. Many ways of forging this link with the congregation could be suggested, but here it is sufficient to note that responsiveness of the parish to suggestions made by the homilist will be in direct proportion to the success or failure of this important preparatory period.

Homilists may be inclined to take the sting out of their messages when sensitive areas are involved. There are times when this is not possible. Bishop Romero, who was assassinated in San Salvador, used the indirect approach until the time came when the abuses in his country were so outrageous that he could no longer afford the luxury of being subtle. There were times when Christ had to make hard choices to upset his listeners. Both Romero and Christ knew they faced death as the result of their decision to attack injustice, but they did not back away from their decision. The individual homilist will need good judgment and frequent prayer to help him determine when easy choices are no longer available. Good homiletic practice includes telling the congregation that Christ brought up difficult topics because he loves us, and that he, the homilist, is obligated to deal with such topics for the same reason. We have never heard of a person who was offended when the homilist stated unabashedly that he loved them, and meant it.

My Responsibility?

The task of suggesting to a congregation what their response should be to critical life situations is a primary responsibility of the homilist. Commercials are masterfully designed to lead to highly specific actions. "Buy this product *now*." Those who sell heroin and cocaine tell their customers these drugs are the answer to loneliness, depression, and feelings of inadequacy. They request action and promise euphoria. They do not deliver, yet they succeed in achieving the response they seek. Once the state lottery was approved in Iowa, the lure of additional income led to the most preposterous ads, telling the public what an enormous mistake they would make if they did not play. If they had only followed their special hunch this week, when the winning numbers made it obvious that if they had used Aunt Anna's birthday and the square root of the age of their eldest grandparent, they would now be millionaires. If not from the pulpit, whence will come the viable alternatives to these messages? The homilist may not find it an easy task to address such issues, but it is a responsibility he cannot lightly turn aside.

Father McGeehan, who objected to making specific requests in his homilies, once remarked, "I simply can't tell my congregation what to do." That may be true, but the homilist should tell them what in his best judgment God wants them to do. The congregation is already being bombarded by every kind of societal force with suggestions of what to do with their time, their resources, their efforts. One of the duties of the ordained minister is to present credible alternatives to the suggestions of society and to document the fact that they are better alternatives.

People continue to express amazement at the continued success of Mother Teresa's religious community. A large part of the explanation for her achievements lies in the fact that she asks great sacrifices of the members. Our own experience is that when we ask parishioners to carry out some kind of action following a homily, the results are in direct proportion to the specificity of the request.

Not Always Something to Be Done

Sometimes the action sought by the homilist may be simply a change in *attitude*. What are the current attitudes of the congregation toward civil rights, the inclusion of women as liturgical ministers, the music program of the parish, the liturgy itself, abortion, child abuse, working long hours for material goods, daily prayer, dishonesty in employer-employee relations, or the parish budget? Do those attitudes vary in any way from those Christ advocated? If they do, it behooves the homilist to suggest changes.

Sometimes the response will be simply one of *praise* and *thanksgiving*, or a decision to *enjoy* the gift of life. As the homilist becomes more precise and suggests courses of action, he will receive verbal responses from the congregation indicating an awareness that action is expected. Both of us have frequently heard responses such as, "Thank you for the encouragement"; "Thanks for having the courage to tell the truth"; "Thank you for saying something my children should hear from me and would have, except that I wasn't brave enough to tell them." There may even be times when the response is "I don't agree with you." At least it is a response, and it offers an opportunity for dialogue.

At Times, No Request Needed

There are times when the message is so direct and explicit that it would be almost redundant to suggest any kind of action.

Frequently this is true in the case of a story to which all members of the congregation can readily relate. Here is an example.

> FF: I told this story on Grandparents' Day to a congregation of children, parents, and grandparents. The homily dealt with the relationship of the elder members of the group to their children and grandchildren.

> My father ran a restaurant, and I used to work for him when I was in grade school and early high school. There was a very large lighted "Coffee Shop" sign hanging over the sidewalk in front of the cafe. The exterior of the sign was beginning to show a bit of wear, and one day my father asked me to repaint it. I had to put up a long ladder on the sidewalk and put sandbags at the bottom of the ladder so it wouldn't slip. I climbed the ladder and looked down. I was afraid of heights, and terrified by the job he had given me, but didn't want to show my fear. The sign was circled with rows of little blue light bulbs that went on and off through some mysterious mechanism I didn't understand. To paint the sign I had to remove all the bulbs. I took up a bushel basket, tied it to the top rung of the ladder, carefully took out all the bulbs one at time and placed them in the basket. I then untied the rope, intending to catch the basket and take it back to the ground. Unfortunately, my hand slipped. The basket fell thirty feet to the sidewalk. I crawled down from my perch, ashen-faced, and examined the bulbs, hoping they would not all be damaged. Every single one was broken. It was depression time, in the 1930s, and the restaurant was not going well. With a heavy heart I went into the shop and told my dad I had broken all the light bulbs. He had only one question: "Did you get hurt?" When I answered no, he said with relief: "Then I'm not worried. I can replace light bulbs. I can't replace a son."

The anecdote is so simple and relevant that it was unnecessary to suggest any kind of action from the parents and grandparents. In fact, it would have spoiled the story to do so.

Not every homily ends with a call for action. On occasion the homilist may simply wish to praise, compliment, console, or affirm. But even these messages, delivered with skill and clarity, will bring about changes in the hearers, especially in their receptiveness to later efforts of the homilist.

Post-Homiletic Suggestion

We would like to suggest a technique that has been found useful when asking someone for action. We call it "post-homiletic suggestion." Psychologists and psychiatrists make use of a procedure known as post-hypnotic suggestion. The hypnotist gives a command to the subject under hypnosis, but instructs the individual to perform the command only when he receives a specific signal after leaving the hypnotized state. The person will then be brought out of hypnosis and will be given the pre-arranged signal that will elicit the particular response asked for by the hypnotist. For example, the hypnotist may tell the person that he will feel revulsion whenever he lights up a cigarette or is given a cocktail.

A similar technique can be applied to homilies. The preacher refers to some specific future action the individual may take and suggests that when the action is considered, the person call to mind an alternative that has been suggested. Here are a few examples.

When you stand on the first tee looking down a beautiful fairway, surrounded by the clubhouse and the swimming pool, say to yourself, "Only a loving God would allow me to enjoy all of this."

When you next drive to work or to the supermarket and feel those knobs on the steering wheel—usually there are ten of them—why not use them to count off a decade of the rosary?

The next time you want to raise your hand to strike your child, think of God's merciful treatment of you.

When you feel blue, when everything seems to be against you, and when God seems far away, ask yourself, "What if I had been born in total poverty, or blind? Would this problem really be that important?"

The technique works. When the members of the congregation next face the circumstances that have been described, the suggestions for action will come into their minds. It is an experiment worth trying.

The thrust of this chapter has been to ask the homilist to avoid generalities, and to remind him that his work is not solely educational. Some kind of response is expected from the congregation. At times, this response may be suggested directly and specifically. At other times, a gentle nudge may be sufficient. On a few occasions, such as the delivery of a meaningful story, the follow-up by the congregation is so evident that no suggestion need be made. In any event, the congregation needs the guidance of the homilist to formulate what their actions should be relative to the message that is found in the readings and given current significance by the homily.

Generalities within a homily have a soporific effect upon the congregation. Specificity is one of the guarantors of interest, involvement, and Christian action. The time allowed for a weekend message is limited—between five and twelve minutes. The homilist needs to take a blue line and strike out every general statement in his homily, then replace it with specific *terms*, specific *examples*, and, when action is called for, specific *actions* expected of the listener who takes the message of the homily to heart.

—9—

Are You Talking to Me?

The homily should speak to the entire congregation

In Chapter 4 we stated that the first job of the homilist is to secure the attention of the congregation; we stressed that the homily must be addressed to the interests of the audience. What we wish to emphasize here is the need to speak to the interests of as many *components* of the congregation as possible. To ensure this, the homilist must know the congregation; he must be aware of the various constituencies among his listeners. Each Sunday he will face an audience that is diverse, yet has many similarities that will make his task easier.

Diverse Congregations

The homilist who studies his congregation at every Sunday liturgy will become aware of the diversity of his listeners. For very good reason the church is called "Catholic," because it includes everyone: men, women, children, the wealthy, the poor, workers, employers, and individuals varying in intelligence from the borderline defective to the genius.

Diversity also exists *between* congregations. Parishes are metropolitan, urban, and rural. Often the location of a parish determines differences in the median age of parishioners, types of occupation, and even political leanings. In metropolitan parishes the income level tends to have a much narrower range than in smaller communities. The majority of families in some parishes are farmers; in others, industrial workers; in still others, professional men and women. The number of college graduates will vary from a few dozen to a majority of the congregation. A similar situation exists in the number of unemployed, the degree of religious training, and a host of other characteristics.

Similarities in a Congregation

Faced with a congregation with quite divergent backgrounds and talents, the homilist may seem to have an almost impossible task. Yet even with these differences there exist in every group identifiable common characteristics, such as shared needs, goals, and problems. We can safely assume that in almost all congregations approximately seventy percent are married, fifty percent are female, a large majority have children or grandchildren. In most parishes there are more grade school children than children attending high school and college.

There are still other similarities, common characteristics, among today's parishioners that may serve as a background for the development of a successful homily. With a few exceptions, today's congregations might be accurately described as follows.

1. *They are well versed in communication.* Most members of modern American parishes have been immersed in communication from the time of their birth. They have been inundated by speeches, writings, dramas, comedies, and ads through radio, television, and a plethora of journals and newsletters. The constant flow of the written and spoken word in their lives has produced a generation of people who are aware of and conditioned to the qualities of good communication. These parishioners are more analytical and perhaps more critical of the homily than were audiences of the past. No longer can the homilist be considered an admired figure just because he stands in the pulpit and delivers a message. Only the best, at least the best the homilist is capable of, is expected. The electrical switch and the television remote control have made it possible for people to turn off messages they have no interest in. Visualize preaching to a congregation, each member of which has a

remote control that could switch off the sound of a boring address from the pulpit. Actually, the members of every congregation have that capacity: They simply tune out in their minds the unwelcome sound of a mediocre or poor homily.

2. *The religious IQ is not high.* Although the average congregation knows the difference between good and poor communication, they are not trained in theology and are not sophisticated in their knowledge about their faith and the church. Today there are fewer graduates of Catholic schools, and the schools themselves place less emphasis on knowledge of the faith than they did in the past. In former days, most Catholic colleges required a course in theology each semester. Today it is a fairly general practice to require the graduate only to sample courses from an academic area that includes both philosophy and religious studies. In addition, those under thirty-five years of age may have little, if any, understanding of the liturgy. Children of Catholic families who have not been taught the meaning of the different elements of the Mass do not find it easy to appreciate the value of the Mass.

The result is that the homilist cannot take for granted the ability of the congregation to follow theological subtleties. He is interested in the correct translation of the Scriptures and the theological meaning of the words of Scripture. Members of the congregation do not have similar training and concerns. Of greater import for them is having a job, and preventing their children's involvement in drugs, sex, and unwholesome groups. They worry about their personal safety and about their salvation. The crowds that followed Jesus did not come to hear him discuss theological concepts, either. They came because they were lame, because they were blind, because they were deaf. They were looking for hope, for consolation, for forgiveness, for meaning in their lives. The average Sunday congregation is not much different. The homilist must be aware of and sensitive to this reality.

3. *They lead busy lives with little time to spare.* The tempo of life has radically changed over the past fifty years. The working day has been shortened, but the hours devoted to other pursuits have been more than filled. The number of organizations one belongs to, the profusion of leisure activities, the opportunities for personal growth and new experiences have multiplied. Men and women often han-

dle two jobs; women are involved in professions in addition to home-making; the lives of children are flooded with sports and other leisure activities. As a result, people guard their time carefully. The day when people would spend a long time visiting with their neighbors after the Sunday service is gone.

4. *They have common needs and desires.* While different age groups and those with different professions have special needs and desires, some might be simply be considered "human" and common to all. The need to belong, the need for autonomy, the need to achieve, the yearning to love and be loved, the desire for health, the desire to live on after death—these and other common aspirations bond an audience in such a way that when the homilist addresses one member about these longings, he addresses nearly all.

5. *They are open and receptive.* The homilist has a receptive audience, people who are open to the Word of God and to hearing how those mysterious, often arcane words of Jesus—and the sometimes even more obscure words of the Old Testament—can make their lives happier and richer. No homilist in touch with his audience can miss the upturned faces, the readiness to learn, and the joy that comes to those who receive insights during the homily that resolve long-standing problems or that provide a turning point in their lives. The receptivity of the congregation is a secret weapon of the homilist. He is not facing a jury daring him to convince them; most are already convinced; they only seek to be enlightened. They are motivated by faith, but even more by hope.

6. *They have been touched by tragedy.* Temporary setbacks, long-time personal problems, and family tragedies are common to every congregation. Not a single individual in the audience has not known adversity of some kind: death or illness, job termination, demotion, business failure, drug dependency, divorce, an unplanned pregnancy, an unhealthy relationship. There is an astonishing number of families in which the members hardly speak to one another. The homilist is in the business of preaching *hope*, the Good News of the Gospel, and he has a marvelous opportunity to convert despair to confidence and discouragement to happiness by giving the congregation insights into God's love for them, what God holds in store for them.

In view of the broad diversity of any given congregation, how is it possible to include all in the homily? Simply by concentrating on what the members of the audience have in common, rather than on the differences. The homilist tries to define what is common in the congregation, and then finds how the Scripture readings for the day relate to one or more of those characteristics.

Including the Entire Congregation

If the homilist keeps in mind that nearly every member of the congregation is at least passively aware of the rules of good communication, is not schooled in the fine points of theological speculation, finds time in short supply, has needs in common with the rest of the congregation, is open and receptive to a good homily, and has been touched at some point in life with tragedy, then the homilist knows much about his audience.

With such knowledge, there are two ways the homilist might include all members of the congregation. The first is by doing just that—including everyone. At various times during a homily, specific references can be made to a particular age group, to married couples, singles, senior citizens, union members, executives, and others. We have already laid the groundwork for this approach by indicating that we must direct our remarks to certain groups if we are to incorporate the first fundamental: *The homily should be of interest to the congregation.* By studying the concerns of individuals in different age brackets, the homilist can quickly refer to three or four groups within a few seconds. Trying to address every category of the parish in every homily would be unwise. Rather, in each homily two or three groups should be specifically included. If the homilist keeps track of the groups that have been mentioned and identifies different groups each Sunday, over a period of a few weeks he will have spoken directly to all. Priests and ministers who use this technique often hear the reaction: "Your homily really touched me personally. How did you know I needed that message?"

Here is how a homilist might include all the members of the congregation when preaching on the Good Samaritan.

Sometimes young people wonder how they might help someone left by the roadside and in need of care. Did you ever consider that at this moment your parents might be pretty discouraged at your conduct around home or your lack of progress in school, and might be wondering whether the sacrifices needed to raise a family are worth it? They might be that someone left wounded by the roadside.

If you are a married person, has your spouse been passed over at work, never getting the anticipated promotion? Is your spouse tied to the home and the children? Does your spouse need a romantic evening and dinner with the one she loves?

Senior citizens have one thing in common: They love to talk. Is there a senior citizen living in your neighborhood whom everyone walks past without seeing the wounds of loneliness and neglect? Could you take a few moments to stop by and listen?

Persons in the congregation have a wonderful capacity for identifying with the characters of a story, especially when the homilist gently suggests the association.

Later on in the homily the speaker may wish to suggest specific action rather than leave the application to the members of the congregation.

For the young people: "When the opportunity arises, if you have the courage to tell your mother that you love her, you are providing her shelter and comfort at the inn."

For the married: "Listen to the subtle indications from your spouse that she or he is hurting and needs someone to care enough to bind the wounds that are suffered each day."

For the lonely senior citizen: "Why not pick up the telephone and call another lonely person? A priest and a levite have already passed him (her) by. You may be the last one to come along."

For all the congregation: "Try to recall one time in your life when God the Father picked you up, wounded, alone, and suffering, and healed you." Or: "The price paid by the Samaritan was generous, but it likely came out of his superfluous funds. The price Christ paid for you was his life blood."

Such references take only sixty to ninety seconds in a homily, but that brief time could make the entire homily meaningful to everyone. Many communicators who have not used this technique before are surprised by the results. Suddenly everyone in the congregation is included in the homily. It really does work!

The second way to include everyone is by directing, at some time during the year, one specific homily toward each segment of the parish: men, women, children, employers, employees, senior citizens, single individuals, etc. Most homilists do this on special occasions, such as Mother's Day, Father's Day, and Catechetical Sunday. At first glance, this method would seem to violate the very principle we have been discussing. Will not the directing of a homily toward one specific group tend to ignore all other groups? Not necessarily. Remarks directed to the youth automatically include all the parents and grandparents, because the comments will include advice those groups are already giving to their children and grandchildren. If the homily includes remarks about drugs, alcohol, or pre-marital sex, the homilist will have the ready attention of all the parents and grandparents in the church, as well as the youth. When directing the homily to the older members of the congregation, the homilist does in some ways include everyone, because every member of the congregation will eventually become part of the older population. Laborers will listen closely to what a homilist says about employers, and vice versa, because they have vital common interests. These connections should be made by the congregation, but it is helpful for the homilist to point out the applications to the various groups in the audience.

Part Three

What the Homilist Must Do

— 10 —

How Much Is a Minute Worth?

You must time your homily properly

The material of this chapter could be summarized by stating: Prepare a good homily, say what you want to say, then sit down. If that takes five minutes, fine. If it takes ten minutes, well and good. But if it takes more than twelve minutes, outside of special occasions, you are in trouble.

Because preaching is usually the principal part of the Protestant liturgy, ministers customarily speak longer than Catholic homilists do. The added time does not change the basic fact that no homily should be delivered until it has been trimmed to remove every irrelevant and unnecessary word, phrase, and sentence. Time is an enormously important topic, in some ways the most significant topic of this book. Congregations will seldom fault a homilist for the brevity of his homily; but even an excellent message, delivered with poise and clarity, can be ruined by an improper use of time.

Precious and Irreplaceable Time

Quoist says in his *Time Prayer*, "We must not lose time, waste time, kill time, for time is a gift that You give us, but a perishable gift, a gift that does not keep." Time is our most precious possession, our only irreplaceable commodity. If someone takes my watch, I can replace it. If someone burns down my home, I can rebuild. But I cannot replace a minute of time that is gone.

Why is it that we seldom give much thought to the priceless value of every moment until perhaps that point in our lives when the doctor gives us the news that the end is just down the road? One answer might be that we live in a world of cycles. Almost everything we experience is cyclic in nature, repetitive. Morning merges into afternoon, afternoon into evening, evening into night, followed with absolute regularity by another morning. Our calendar year is cyclic, as are the seasons. The tides of the oceans, the spinning of the planetary bodies, all follow that measured flow we call the cyclic rhythm.

Time follows a different course. Time is a straight line, beginning for each of us at a dim, distant moment whose factual origin is disputed, and ending at an equally unpredictable moment when that mysterious spark of life leaves the human body. However, since we live in a cyclic world in which we do usually return to the starting point, we tend to place time in the same conceptual framework.

Finite Time

In addition to being irreplaceable, time has another restrictive quality: It is limited; it is scarce. There is something about creation in general that prevents us from adverting to this characteristic of time. That factor is the vastness of the universe, the boundless nature of space and matter. In these days of celestial exploration, when scientists describe the distance between Earth and stellar bodies, those distances are so great and matter so profuse that we have to use terms like "light years" just to try to bring the vastness of creation into some kind of understandable terms. We describe the age of the universe not in thousands or millions of years, but in billions. We are so dazzled with the huge numbers scientists hurl at us that we tend to lose sight of the finite things of life. One of them is time. Only the death of a close friend or relative shatters our concept of the near-infinity of time and jolts us back to the awareness that some things are not measured in light years.

Preparing Means Paring
Archbishop McNicholas, Ordinary of the Archdiocese of Cin-

cinnati during the 1940s, was noted for the brevity as well as for the quality of his homilies. His secretary once revealed that McNicholas would work for many hours on every message and would revise it as many as ten or twelve times until he finally had on paper exactly what he wanted to say and *no more*. When the address was delivered, the hard work was evident to all his listeners. Each message was precise, crisp, to the point; and none of them, even on the most solemn occasion, lasted more than seven minutes.

> FF: Msgr. Kerper, the pastor of a large parish in Dubuque, Iowa, would not tolerate in himself or in his associate pastors a lack of preparedness for a homily that might result in wasted minutes in the pulpit. On the first weekend that I served at the parish, he approached me on Saturday evening (before the time when Saturday evening Masses were allowed) and said, "You will offer the eleven and the twelve o'clock Masses tomorrow. You will preach at both. You will preach for four minutes." I protested, "But, Monsignor, no one can preach a homily in four minutes." The reply was, "Not unless you prepare."

Both McNicholas and Kerper were keenly aware that whenever they preached or read a letter or made announcements from the pulpit, they had a captive audience. They conveyed to their associates a realization that improperly using the time of another is a matter of conscience: Thou shalt not steal. The time of another person is so precious and limited that if I misuse that time I am stealing just as surely as if I took his watch or car or her purse or ring.

Stealing Time

Just how much is a minute worth? Suppose I have prepared a homily for the Sunday liturgy that will take twelve minutes to deliver. Through careful revision I could remove repetitions, unnecessary words and side excursions, and reduce the homily to nine minutes. If I fail to save those three minutes, and if there are 1000 people in the church, I have stolen 3000 minutes. That amounts to fifty hours, six work days, almost a full week of work time. No one has the right to waste that kind of time.

Wouldn't it be an interesting situation if every speaker judged his talk with the seventh commandment in mind, with the thought that he must not abuse his power over a captive audience? If that were to take place, one of two things would happen: Talks would get shorter, or the confessional lines would get longer.

Father James Swetnam sent us the following story. Some years ago in Washington, D.C., people in one parish complained constantly about an assistant priest. The bishop, weary of hearing the complaints, finally removed him and sent as a replacement an assistant who gave homilies averaging forty-five minutes in length. He was immediately given the nickname "The Bishop's Revenge."

Brevity itself is not the principal issue here. The issue is the value of time, the worth of each minute. If twenty minutes are needed to deliver a message, twenty minutes should be used. We are simply saying that any unnecessary expenditure of time within the homily is an inexcusable violation of the rights of the audience; we are advising the elimination of the superfluous and expendable.

Here is an example:

Jesus went from Bethlehem to Jerusalem, a distance of about five miles. He was riding a donkey, which was a common mode of transportation at the time. There were many date palm trees in the area, and I'm sure many of you who have visited the Holy Land remember seeing them. When Jesus arrived in Jerusalem, he entered the city through the southern gate and went directly to the Temple. There he began to teach the people.

There are seventy-seven words in that paragraph. There are occasions when the addition of such details may help the congregation to understand the message of the homily, but ordinarily this type of paragraph should be re-written to save time and increase interest.

Jesus went from Bethlehem to Jerusalem and went directly to the Temple. There he began to teach the people.

The same information has been given in nineteen words, a saving of fifty-eight unnecessary words. The donkey, the date palms, and the south gate have no bearing on the message; they have nothing to do with either the topic or the objective, and so they confuse the message. While the homilist was speaking those unnecessary words, he was signaling his audience to stop paying attention. And undoubtedly they obliged.

Varying the Length

Some preachers have the reputation of always giving a five-minute homily, and set up expectations in the congregation, which later interfere when a longer or shorter homily is appropriate. Although their homilies might be excellent, the regularity of timing runs the risk of leading the parishioners to conclude that the preacher does not consider any topic important enough to spend more than five minutes discussing it. It is a mistake to speak consistently for either a long or a short period. It will be obvious to the congregation that some topics simply cannot carry the burden of a twelve-minute discourse, while others can only be touched on in that period of time. Homilies that run, from Sunday to Sunday, exactly eight or nine or ten minutes offer no variety.

Thus far we have discussed the importance of paring unneeded words, phrases, and examples from a homily. The point was not to work toward a brief homily, but to bring about clarity and simplicity in the message. Is there a value in brevity itself? We believe that sometimes there is. A good example is the daily homily. It was never the intention of the revised liturgy to encourage the delivery on weekdays of the same complete message that can be expected for the weekends. In North America a large number of business men and women make a serious attempt to begin their work day by attending the liturgy. Their schedule in most cases is not flexible; they need to be at the office at 8:00 or 8:15, or whenever the workday begins. Careful use of time in the planning and execution of the liturgy is simply a courteous recognition of the time constraints placed on people who wish to combine their workday with worship.

Length and Quality

There is no correlation between quality and the length of a

homily. Preachers may well take a lesson from Abraham Lincoln. The Gettysburg Address is one of the finest pieces of oral communication in American history. The entire address consisted of only 262 words. The average delivery of a homily at moderate speed will cover approximately 140 words a minute. Even with pauses for emphasis, Lincoln's address did not consume much more than two minutes. The speech is carved on the walls of the Lincoln Memorial in Washington, D.C., and one can often observe visitors reading the words, spellbound by the beauty, the simplicity, and the depth of that gem of communication. Lincoln's appearance was preceded by that of Edward Everett, former president of Harvard University and Senator from Massachusetts. Everett was one of the finest orators in the country. He spoke for nearly two hours, giving a brilliant resume of the battle of Gettysburg. Everett later wrote to Lincoln, "I should be glad if I could flatter myself that I came as near the central idea of the occasion in two hours as you did in two minutes."

Those who regularly exceed the appropriate amount of time for a homily should give thought to trying a brief homily on occasion, if for no other reason than for the discipline it brings to writing.

FF: Bishop Francis Dunn, noted for his kindness and humility but also for his lengthy and peripatetic homilies, once asked me for suggestions how he might be more effective on his confirmation tour. I recommended that he take a sheet of 8.5 by 11 paper and cut it in two. Then I asked him to put the half sheet in the typewriter and begin to put his thoughts down for a homily. If he came to the end of the sheet and the homily was not completed, he was saying too much, had included extraneous matter, or was repeating himself. He was to put another half sheet in and try again; when the homily was completed at the end of the sheet, it was ready to be delivered. The bishop tried the system, and within a few weeks reports were coming in from around the diocese about the wonderful talks he was giving. His talks were wonderful not because they were brief, but because in seeking brevity he gained clarity of thought and precision of expression.

This man improved his homilies because he realized they were not maximally effective; he was willing to ask for advice, accept it, and make the necessary changes.

The homilist can also learn from the marketplace. Many people believe that the 1988 presidential election was won by twenty- to thirty-second utterances on TV commonly known as sound bytes.

If the homilist wishes to verify the value of brevity, he need only conduct a survey of his congregation on any given Sunday, asking two questions: "Will those who think the homilies are too short please raise their hands? . . . Now will all those who think the homilies are too long please raise their hands?" While preparing the material for this book, the authors frequently mentioned to lay people some of the ideas to be included in the book. Almost universal was the response, "Are you going to ask homilists to be brief?" The regularity of such a comment should be a message to all speakers. There are times when the liturgy is so powerful that a homily is unnecessary. The Easter Vigil is an example.

Somewhere in a book on homiletics written by a Protestant clergyman, we read this thought, "Self-imposed conservation adds weight to what you say." We agree wholeheartedly. Words are the dominant factor that determines the length of a homily.

After the Homily

How we use the time *following* the homily is also important. It is quite appropriate and liturgically recommended to pause for a few moments after the homily before proceeding with the Creed. However, as is true of the homily itself, the expenditure of that time must be meaningful if it is to be beneficial to the congregation. If the parishioners have no idea why they are now sitting down, other than the fact that the pastor has taken his position at the presider's chair, they will look upon that period as down time. The pause is a perfect time to reflect on the call to action, or to the change of attitude suggested in the homily. If the presider says, "Think about how much God has given us" or makes the suggestion, "Consider for a few moments in silence how we would have acted as the parent of the Prodigal Son," or gives *any* kind of directive for using the silent period, it can be a fruitful and prayerful time for the parishioners.

EM: It is not possible to give an example of a perfectly timed homily, because circumstances dictate the length of any homily. However, I recall a homily that I thought was appropriately timed. It happened in July in Litchfield, Illinois. My wife and six of our children attended the 11:00 Mass. The temperature was ninety-eight degrees, and the church had neither fans nor air conditioning. After the Gospel, the celebrant paused, his eyes scanned the congregation, and he said, "I'm sorry I don't have a lengthy homily for you today; it's too hot. Just think for a moment what hell must be like. . . . Let us pray the Creed."

— 11 —

There Is No Other Way

You must prepare and organize your homily

Developing a good homily requires prayer, study, consultation, and careful, thorough preparation. Every speaker approaches this task from his own individual background, and so the particular elements of preparing and organizing a homily cannot be specified as precisely as can those of some of the fundamentals already discussed. However, there are constants in this step just as there are in the others. We shall discuss some of the basic procedures for both remote and proximate preparation.

Remote Preparation

We suggest that the homilist not prepare Sunday by Sunday, but rather in periods of approximately four weeks at a time. The purpose of this is to provide variety for a series of homilies—an important key in maintaining the interest of the audience week after week. The homilist begins by reviewing the readings for the next four Sundays. Then, each Sunday, he studies the readings of the fourth Sunday from that date, and repeats the process every week. By doing so he begins to formulate ideas, goals, and objectives for the month ahead. The speaker who uses this type of preparation will broaden and deepen his remote preparation for each presentation. Further, by having in mind the objective and topic of the next four homilies, he will subconsciously begin to prepare for each of them well in advance. Ideas that come to mind will be catalogued and will become pre-homiletic suggestions.

Every speaker is aware of what happens in the subconscious the night before an address is to be given. The talk is fairly well outlined; then related thoughts begin to churn through the mind in the evening and after retiring. There are last-minute insights even during sleep that can perceptibly improve a talk already well organized and prepared. It is well to keep a pencil and pad of paper, or a small tape recorder, at hand on the desk, at the bedside, and in the car so that those post-writing thoughts do not escape. This ruminating process can be used to even greater advantage when the speaker has determined the topics and the specific objectives for the homilies of the next four weeks. The topics become like a piece of music recently heard that keeps resonating in the mind long after the sound has died away.

A variety of ideas will surface; some will be discarded, others will be put on the back burner, and still others will emerge as central themes for the individual homilies. The mind will subconsciously attract and catalogue every random thought. If these thoughts have a bearing on the homilies planned for future delivery, they can be jotted down for recall at the time of proximate preparation. The key in this process is to know the topic and objective of the homilies for the next several weeks. Without that key, intervening experiences or thoughts lack relevance, and so the mind has no track on which to run. Homilists who use this method report that ideas will pop into their heads as they watch television, read the newspaper, counsel a parishioner, or drive a car. The procedure does not require more time overall for homily preparation. On Monday morning, instead of starting at ground zero for next Sunday's homily, sixty percent of the work will already be completed.

Remote preparation will also include the use of data files, a review of homilies already given, and the reading of current literature as well as biblical articles and books, but not homiletic services. We shall say a word about these services in the discussion of proximate preparation.

The Steps in Proximate Preparation

There are two general methods of preparing a homily. For the sake of exposition, we shall call one "Method A" and the other "Method B." Each begins with a review of the readings and the development of an outline. At this point is found the only real divergence. The issue is whether to use an outline as the final document, Method A, or to write and use a manuscript, Method B. Again, the steps that *follow* the development of an outline or a manuscript are identical. Both A and B are acceptable techniques. The individual homilist will select the method best suited to his personal style.

1. Review the readings for the liturgy. Having determined on the basis of the readings what are to be the topics and objectives of the various homilies for the coming four weeks in a general way, the homilist will begin work on the homily for the coming Sunday. The readings should be studied thoroughly until the goal, objective, topic, and interest factor have been determined.

Both a topic and a specific objective will usually be suggested by the readings themselves, or perhaps by a current need of the parish for which the readings have particular relevance. Fasten upon a sentence or an idea in the readings and expand that to develop the message. Once this has been accomplished, the most difficult portion of the work has been completed.

The homilist should stay on a single topic, rather than wander through all the readings, doing exegesis. He should also keep in mind the goal of the homily. Is your purpose today to motivate, to educate, to inspire, to rebuke, to praise, to cheer up, or to call for action?

2. Prepare an outline. Few steps in the preparation of a homily discipline the mind, clarify thought, and sharpen the direction of a homily more than developing an outline. An outline forces you to think in an organized fashion about the contents of the homily and the relationships among ideas. Often it reveals subject matter that is extraneous and should be deleted. Listing the topic, objective, and goal at the top of the page can be helpful.

3. Prepare a manuscript. At this point we find the only difference between the two methods of developing the homily. The homilist who adopts Method A will not prepare a manuscript. For many speakers, preaching from a well-prepared outline rather than a script has distinct advantages. It avoids a mechanical recitation of the homily; it opens up for the homilist the possibility of utilizing insights that may come during the delivery; it affords an opportunity for responding to audience feedback.

Other preachers are more successful and feel more comfortable using Method B with their final document in manuscript form rather than relying on an outline. The technique is acceptable as long as the script is not read. The text should be used only as a guide for faulty memory, and as a fallback position when the precise word or phrase desired does not come to mind. In oral communication, the homilist must not give the audience the impression that what he is presenting is canned, but rather that these are *his* views, *his* method of applying Christ's words to the problems and concerns of the congregation. To do that, he must seem natural and not woodenly read a homily.

Nevertheless, it *is* possible to use a manuscript in the pulpit with success, if the homily has been committed to memory, so that eye contact with the audience and naturalness in delivery are not excluded. Manuscripts are used by speakers who feel somewhat uncomfortable with the extemporaneous style of speaking called for by talking from an outline, and who are inclined to convey their ideas through specific, carefully chosen words and phrases for which they judge there is no substitute. At this point, the follower of Method B will prepare his first draft of the homily, with the understanding that it may be only the first of many.

One advantage in the use of a written script is that it tends to facilitate the use of proper transitions. These key elements in a presentation are the guides that make it possible for the audience to follow the direction of the message. The use of precise transitional sentences or clauses when there is a change in the direction of the homily is absolutely essential. The speaker knows that a new point is being made, or a new subject is being introduced; the hearer does not. Such practices as enumerating the points of a homily, "first," "second," "third," or using connective phrases such as, "In addition to . . . I would like to add," or, "So much for the political issues involved; we now turn to . . ." are helpful to the congregation in understanding the flow of the presentation. Transitions, and, more important, the lack thereof, are easier to spot in a manuscript than in an outline. The homilist who prefers to work from an outline should write transitions between points and sub-points of the outline, and use them at the appropriate times.

4. *Add elements for audience relevance.* An outline has been developed, and possibly the first draft of a manuscript. Now the message is fleshed in. References to the lives of various groups in the congregation make the homily interesting to everyone. Included should be specific illustrations the audience can relate to and, where possible, examples that are relevant to the various age groups and those with different professional callings.

The structure of a homily may be compared to that of a building. The edifice has been framed, but now it must be completed. Personal stories will add a distinctive touch. The building is given color by quotations from Scripture, from literature, from the day's newspaper. The other portions of the structure will be references that include the entire audience, human interest stories, and biblical quotations. The interior decoration of the homily is fashioned to fit the needs of the individual family, the congregation facing the speaker.

5. *Endings and beginnings are significant.* Mainline rhetorical theory divides the oral discourse into three major parts: the introduction, the body, and the conclusion. Each of these three parts has a distinct function. The introduction, or beginning, should be designed to gain the attention of the hearers. The body or middle develops the topic, and the ending brings together all that has been presented in the discourse. However, the homilist should seldom prepare his homily in that same order. First in occurrence does not mean first in preparation. The concern of the homilist is to know exactly where he is heading with his topic and how best to get there. The golfer on a par three hole must know where the flag is before addressing the ball. The first step for any trip is to decide where the traveler is going. The destination determines the preparation for the golfer and the traveler. Several of the chapters of this book address the preparation of the body of the homily; here we are concerned with the beginning and the end.

6. *Begin your preparation with the conclusion.* For the homilist, the preparation must begin with a preview of what he wants of the congregation. How do you wish them to apply a passage of

Scripture to their daily lives? Only when you know what you will ask of them can you begin to develop your topic. Only when you know what action you will call them to can you know what sort of conclusion will be needed to do that. Often a passage from one of the readings will be the most fitting conclusion, summarizing in a nutshell all that you have said in the homily. Perhaps you will have a quotation from literature or a well-respected speaker, a quotation that will bring together all the major points of the homily. Perhaps a simple review of what you have said will be the best way to end. The passage, the quotation, the summary must be your starting point as it outlines or suggests what you need to include and what to omit in your homily.

The conclusion is the emotional apogee of any discourse. From ancient times, rhetoricians have written of the importance of an affective appeal in the ending as the most successful way of making the message memorable and persuasive. Consistent with this, another chapter has been devoted to the call for specific action in the conclusion.

Like any climax, the emotional aspect of the conclusion must be built up gradually, and then must be left to do its own work without further comment. Does God add a further word to the sunset? Does the effective lawyer ask one question too many? No, in both cases, and no for the homilist. You must know when to stop. And that stopping point *is* the well-prepared conclusion. Father Joe, who seems to have had an aversion to finishing a homily, was once described as a priest "who lacks terminal facilities."

Comparable to the emotional close is the vivid illustration, one that evokes an image in full living color in the minds of the listeners. The illustration should bring together all the arguments and feelings you conveyed during the homily.

The recommended time spent on a conclusion is not more than ten percent of your total speaking time: short and to the point. That means you have to hone and re-hone your conclusion; write it out and work it with as much care as you would to perfect a short poem. Your conclusion is effective if it is recalled as the congregation leaves the church, as they talk during dinner, as they go about their duties the next day.

The last *sentence* of the homily is the most important sentence of the entire message. It is an expression of the heart of the message in encapsulated form. Because it is last, it will likely be the sentence best remembered by the congregation. We often spend more time on the last sentence than on the main portion of the homily. Here is an example from a homily delivered on the thirty-first Sunday of the year, B Cycle, using only the final portion of the manuscript. The reading was the story of the scribe who asked Jesus what was the first of all the laws.

Jesus answered that there were two: love of God and love of neighbor. The scribe then makes a surprising statement to the effect that love of God and neighbor is more important than any burnt offering or sacrifice. In modern language that is equivalent to saying that love of God and neighbor is more important than going to church. Even more surprising, Jesus assents to this conviction. He was not saying that attending the liturgy was unimportant, only that no one should ever substitute liturgy for the obligation to love God and neighbor. How easy it is for us to attend every liturgical celebration, say the rosary, morning and evening prayers, then ignore the needs of the poor, the sick, and the lonely. Yet Jesus is telling us in the Gospel: "When you have paid your respects to God the Father, you have only begun."

7. *Complete your preparation with the introduction.* This portion of the homily should be addressed *after* the body of the homily is known. Only after you know how you will develop your topic and where it will take you can you effectively design a beginning that will lead your parishioners into the topic. The primary purpose of the introduction is, first and foremost, to gain the attention, arouse the interest, excite the curiosity of the assembly. If you presume the faith and good will of all the congregation members, you may be speaking only to a select few of the already converted, short-changing your mission as a homilist and impeding the Holy Spirit's activity. Speaking to a captive audience does not mean you have their undivided attention. If the Spirit is to be effective through you, you have to do your part.

The two methods of beginning the homily that are least effective are, unfortunately, the two methods most often used in the pulpit: a mere announcement of the topic, and the asking of a rhetorical question. Both techniques take for granted that before you begin to speak, the listeners have a burning desire to hear exactly what you will say on this particular topic.

Perhaps you do not think you are merely announcing your topic, but you are if you limit your introduction to "The readings for today . . ." or, "St. John tells us . . ." Recall your own days, perhaps, as a student when a professor announced that today he would cover the chapter on Maslow's hierarchy of needs. A title or its announcement is important in flyers, books, and library cards; in a homily it belongs on the top of your notes or manuscript, and should not be part of your delivery.

The rhetorical question can be a very effective beginning if, and only if, it is a powerful attention-getter. If you were to ask the congregation whether they wish to know the exact numbers for the winning lotto next Saturday, you would have an exciting question. If you ask them how they can love their neighbor, you do not have an interesting beginning. It would be better to dig deeper into more effective techniques for your introduction.

The Gospel writers had an excellent beginning technique for every portion of the reading: a human interest story. It is a device the homilist can use to gain attention. "Last Wednesday, after a long and difficult day, just as I was ready to go to sleep, the phone rang. A voice on the other end . . ." "Mrs. Janis, who lives in another parish told me that she was thrilled when . . ." With a start like this, the assembly is all ears. We love to hear a story about one of us. The story should lead into your topic either directly or indirectly, with a twist that makes the transition.

Paying the members of the congregation a compliment is certain to gain attention. We all like to be stroked, and we pay attention to those who think we do well. The compliment must, of course, be true, and related to your topic.

Referring to a recent incident the listeners are familiar with asks them to identify with your homily, since it suggests they are in the know. It is a sure way to generate interest. However, the recent incident must be known to all, otherwise you create insiders and outsiders, alienating a portion of your audience.

Using a quotation the parishioners can identify with is effective for capturing interest. But it can be tricky; our society drifts more and more away from literature and refined writing. In addition to its value for gaining attention, and for suggesting an outline for your approach to the topic, the quotation can add credibility to you as a homilist, since you identify with the values shared by your parishioners. Quoting Scripture can be an effective beginning, but should be used with even greater care. Familiarity with Scripture is a goal not yet attained by most parishioners.

A special use of the quotation is one that is begun in the introduction and completed or fulfilled in the conclusion. This technique ties the homily together and enhances your credibility, for it says that you spent considerable time thinking about your hearers and preparing your homily. The following portion of a homily (Thirteenth Sunday, B Cycle) provides an example:

There is a profound lesson to be found in these words from our first reading: "God did not make death, nor does he rejoice in the destruction of the living. For God fashioned all things that they might have being." Being, that is, having life, is at the very heart of God's nature. When Moses encountered God speaking from the burning bush, Moses asked him his name. And the answer was: "This is my name: I am who am." He was telling Moses: "The most significant thing about me is that I exist. I always did and always will. I live. Not like a stone or a piece of metal; those things exist; but I live. I have life." That is the meaning of "I am who am. . . ."

Two further thoughts about this reading. First, if indeed death is repugnant to God, then the astonishing fact that God permitted the Son to die on the cross was a supreme act of love. Secondly, since the world was created by a God who is committed to life, then life must win out in the end. Death may intervene as a temporary state, but it cannot possibly represent a final condition in the plan of a God whose every act is life-giving. Something to think about for those who have lost a loved one. "God did not make death, nor does God rejoice in the destruction of the living. For God fashioned all things that they might have being."

The introduction, like the conclusion, should not exceed ten percent of your total speaking time. If it is long, you risk putting too much emphasis on a minor aspect of your topic, and risk losing much of the impact of your message.

Final Steps

The main elements of preparation have been completed. The final steps provide refinements, clarity and, quite often, reductions in length.

1. Dictate into a recorder. The speaker is now ready for the second draft of the homily, whether the draft is merely mental, a sketchy outline, or a written document. At this point we recommend that the homily be dictated into a tape recorder. This first draft will not be one that is eventually used. It is a trial balloon. It is the first oral sketch of the homily.

2. Listen and change. Since the audience must listen to the homily, the homilist should now do the same. Listening to the tape will give a great deal of information on the completeness of thought, the appropriateness of word choice, the clarity of expression and, an absolutely key point, whether the homilist has prepared an *aural* or a *visual* document.

Let us explain. With reference to those we wish to communicate with, there are two basic modes of presentation: an aural presentation is one that is meant to be listened to; a visual communication is meant to be read. An aural message avoids expressions such as homonyms, which confuse the audience because it cannot distinguish by hearing between two words with different meanings but identical sounds (for example, bore and boar); it avoids alliteration except for carefully selected phrases; it leads the listener from topic to topic by a judicious use of transitional words and phrases; it uses specific words to evoke mental pictures; it employs words that imitate the natural sound associated with the action or object (buzz, rip, chickadee); and it is most effective when it comes across as a piece of conversation. Aural language is used by television and radio announcers and by public speakers of every kind. This type of presentation is pleasing to the ear. Aural presentations *sound* good, although they may not look good in print.

Visual communication does not need to avoid homonyms; it

makes use of punctuation, headings, and paragraph structure to inform readers when a change in direction is being taken; it emphasizes the smooth flow of words; it is meant to please the eye, trained to view the printed page. Visual communication is used by writers of books and articles.

After hearing the tape of his homily, the speaker should review the outline and make appropriate changes. By this time ninety percent of the personal preparation is completed. You have determined the interest factor, identified a goal, topic, and objective, have prepared an outline and, perhaps, a manuscript. You have developed specific references that will be of interest to the audience, and have asked the congregation, when appropriate, to take some action.

3. *Search for the precise words*. In nearly every sentence of an address, the speaker will be faced with the challenge of finding exactly the right words. Time spent in substituting words should not be considered a waste. Precision of words brings clarity to a homily, gives it sparkle and elegance, adds balance and a pleasant sound. The audience will resonate to every effort on the part of the speaker to inject these elements into his message.

FF: I recall an afternoon spent with Father Raymond Roseliep, one of the fine poets of Iowa. He had nearly completed a new poem in which, at one point, the verse portrayed a team of horses coming down a wooden cobblestone street. He was searching for an onomatopoeic word to describe both the movement and the sound of the horses. He had selected and discarded a dozen words; among those not considered as accurately depicting the scene were: dancing, prancing, trotting, and many others. After about two hours, I suggested the word "thudding," and Roseliep nearly leapt for joy. It was the only word in the English vocabulary that expressed exactly what he wanted to say in that line.

The acquisition of a vocabulary that makes possible the selection of the right word for every situation can come from a regular and broad reading of literature, especially poetry. In addition, there are two tools the writer can use to develop a sensitivity to precise and appropriate expressions. One is the crossword puzzle; the other is the thesaurus. Daily exercises in the first trains the mind to search actively for adequate substitute words; the use of the second provides a tool for finding such words. We recommend both.

4. *Check timing.* A homily should be timed only to make sure it is not too long. If the recommended procedures have been followed carefully, there should be no need to examine the timing. If the delivery takes five minutes, or ten or even twelve, that is fine. Say everything that has to be said. Everything, but no more! The homilist should always bear in mind the importance of not abusing time. For this reason, the homily should be read or spoken aloud carefully with the intention of excluding every extraneous word, phrase, and sentence. All speakers and writers will on occasion come up with gems of thought that would be delightful to use in a homily. But if they are irrelevant, they must be sacrificed. Any other choice is a violation of the rights of the congregation, an abuse of a captive audience. Write down and save those gems for another time.

5. *Finalize the written product.* This is the last step, the most immediate preparation of the homily. The homilist should not be afraid of doing this "last" step several times. Almost every session given to a practice delivery of the homily will result in desirable changes in either the outline, the script, or both. Father Clarence Friedman used to say that every preacher has three presentations for a Sunday homily: The first is the one he prepares; the second, the one he gives; and the third, the one he should have given—if he had prepared just a little more.

How much time will all of this take? Initially, because it is new, it will take longer than the usual writing of a Sunday homily. However, after only a few weeks, the preparation for the homily will become exciting and challenging, and the time needed to complete the process will be shortened.

Group Preparation

One preparation technique that has proved to be successful is to have a monthly meeting of a group of priests, deacons, or ministers to discuss the significance of the readings without the actual preparation of a homily. Still another variant is to work with another person while preparing the homily.

FF: One of the most productive periods in the preparation of homilies in my ministry happened during the lifetime of Father Clarence Friedman, whose name has already been mentioned in this book. We were stationed in neighboring parishes. Father Friedman was a voracious reader and a precise thinker with a magnificent imagination. He was a master at developing ideas for the Sunday homily, but occasionally found difficulty compressing them into a practical message. I seemed able to tame Friedman's thoughts and work them into an outline. We formed a symbiotic relationship and worked together as a team on homilies. We would call one another during the week, and over the telephone develop the basic outline for next Sunday's homily. I often said to him, to his delighted amusement, "You furnish the thunderbolts, and I will harness them for you." Such a relationship may come only once in a lifetime, but if it does, the homilist would be well advised to take advantage of it.

Homiletic Services?

Homiletic services can be helpful; they can suggest examples and illustrations. They cannot replace prayer, study, and work. The use of these documents should be postponed until the last stages of proximate preparation. Completely prepare the initial draft. After you have made an outline and recorded the first version of the message, but before outlining the final draft, check with your favorite homiletic service. You may find some excellent ideas and examples that you can incorporate into the homily. But avoid the practice of those homilists who use someone else's words and try to pass them off to the congregation as their own. Most congregations are very perceptive and will immediately recognize the photocopied sermon.

— 12 —

All the World Is Not a Stage

You must be yourself to be believable

For the Hebrew people of Old Testament times, the beginning of wisdom was the fear of the Lord. For the Greeks, the initial step for those seeking to become wise was self-knowledge. One of the most quoted of all Greek expressions is "Know thyself." This aphorism was inscribed in letters of gold on the temple of Apollo at Delphi. It asserted that knowledge of self is a starting point without which other advances in wisdom have a flimsy foundation. Poets, philosophers, and psychologists have declared that self-knowledge is difficult to acquire, primarily because there is less objectivity in making judgments about self than in the perception of data outside the self. The Freudian concept of the arcane unconscious supports such a conclusion.

The flip side of this admonition, and a *sine qua non* for the homilist, is "Be thyself." To act consistent with one's basic characteristics is fundamental in successful communication. A speaker cannot be effective with an audience if he or she does not cast an image of credibility. One of the keys to that credibility is the projection of oneself, not another, to the audience. The two tasks, "Know yourself" and "Be yourself" are intimately related. The discussion to follow will be restricted to the second task: "Be yourself."

The first is a preliminary that will be presumed to have been achieved by the homilist.

There are certain skills that can be used in making a person believable. The con artist has achieved credibility through tone of voice, facial expressions, and glib argumentation. The talented writer uses precise words and well-turned sentences. High achievers in business, architecture, law, or medicine cast a spell of believability because of their success in the field; they have a track record. The homilist, even if he lacks the talents of the con artist, the trained writer, and the professional leader, has access to one skill people always respond to: he can be himself. Genuineness and authenticity beget credibility.

Shouldn't Everyone Believe a Priest or Minister?

Not all homilists are priests or ministers, but for the moment we shall restrict our remarks to those who are. The question is legitimate. There was a time when the word of these individuals was rarely questioned. They were the best educated people in the community. Their judgment on almost any topic was respected. That day is gone.

In today's society, the credibility of priests has been subjected to particular stress. Changes in church teaching and in the liturgy have had an unsettling effect upon many, and caused people to wonder whether the church and its clergy know where they are going. Another possible reason for a decline in the believability of the clergy was that many who had stressed to couples their obligation of fidelity to their vocation left the priesthood and married. Others, during a fortunately brief but tragic period in the history of Catholic high school education, weakened the faith of adolescents by declaring that the Sunday obligation was excused for the simplest of reasons. Finally, the human weaknesses priests share with everyone else have, in recent years, been exposed to the glare of national publicity, and have even been brought into the courtroom. All these factors have led to a decline in both the authority and the believability of the clergy.

The public has become wary of advisors on *every* level. Many trusted in Richard Nixon and were disappointed. Some had confidence in Tammy and Jim Bakker and were saddened. Some believed that their government would cut spending, increase job opportunities, and provide a social security system that would give them a safe retirement program; they were disappointed in their leaders and have become disenchanted. Authorities in any field are no longer automatically believed. In fact, a deadening cynicism toward leaders, not limited to the young, has infected our nation.

People require more credibility from the priest than from almost any other authority figure. If a stockbroker gives bad advice, clients lose their funds. If a priest does the same, parishioners may lose what is more important; they include such things as self-respect, peace of mind, even faith.

How Does a Homilist Become Believable?

In the face of such widespread distrust of authority figures, how does the homilist achieve credibility? There are several ways.

1. *By being himself.* The first and most important requirement for establishing credibility is for the homilist to be himself. In many ways, the pulpit may seem like a stage: up front, elevated, all eyes focused on it. Often, homilists react to the pulpit as if they were walking up to the footlights, preparing to perform. Fearing their ability to do an adequate job, they take on another identity. But the pulpit is not a stage; the homilist is not an actor. He cannot be someone he is not.

EM: My eldest daughter, Mary Ann, put her finger on the problem. We were discussing homilies one evening when she said, "Priests come into our home for a visit on Saturday night and they are ordinary human beings. They laugh, they discuss current topics, they ask questions, and are just 'normal.' I like them. The next day I hear them in the pulpit and they are serious, dead-panned, talk in language I've never heard them use, and generally become a different person. They are boring. I'm confused. I don't know who's talking to me. What happens to them?"

They are acting, of course. And acting is a very difficult profession. Great skill, a lifetime of training, and an incredible amount of talent in the field of mimicry is required for someone to take on another's personality. Priests do not ordinarily have that training; even if they did, acting does not succeed in the pulpit because the parishioners know their homilists from daily contacts. Even skilled actors cannot "act" in the company of their close friends, who know their real personalities. If the homilist has served a parish for at least a few months, the congregation knows his moods, his likes and dislikes, and his idiosyncrasies. They will recognize an "act" in a moment.

Why then, if acting is both difficult and ineffective, do speakers often project a different image when speaking before a group? For some, perhaps, the unspoken and even unrealized intention is self-protection. Fear of failure is a significant factor in the lives of priests. One can discern signs of it, in both young and old clergy, in the sometimes casual and even brash approach to highly volatile subjects, an unwillingness to listen to opinions that vary from their own convictions, and the shortness of fuse when someone even mildly suggests that they may have made an error in judgment. When we fear failure, we are quick to put on a mask to cover our concern. If we should fail, it is not really we who have blundered, but the mask we have worn, the person whose identity we have adopted. But the chances for success are enhanced if the homilist projects his true personality when communicating a message. For *that* is the person, not the substitute created by acting, who has committed his life to the service of people. *That* is the person, not another, who has been appointed spiritual director of this congregation. *That* is the person who, after the Sunday liturgy, will be living the messages of the homily with the people.

Clyde Fant writes (*Preaching for Today*, p. 60):

After honesty, naturalness [believability] is the second requirement for true humanity. Naturalness means not adding to or subtracting from your personality. Some men (and women) try to be more than they are; they want to appear holier, or more profound, or more dynamic. Others are scared to death to seem to be as much as they are; they do not want to be regarded as zealous or devout. Both project a false, unnatural personality.

2. By his use of language. The homilist often deviates from his real character in his choice of verbal expressions. He will use words and expressions in his homily totally unlike his everyday conversation. Phrases such as "Holy Mother the Church," "Christ, our Shepherd King," "The Word Incarnate," or "down through the ages," are seldom a part of daily discussions. When these expressions are found in a homily the preacher is saying, "This is not really me in the pulpit. I use these words and phrases only to impress you." They may be correct theological terms, but they belong in a textbook. The audience will know that the homilist who uses them is speaking out of character. (There *are* priests who do talk that way in daily conversation, and they are the dullest speakers we know.) The Bishops' Committee on Priestly Life and Ministry states: "The New Testament usage suggests that a homily should sound more like a personal conversation, albeit a conversation on matters of utmost importance, than like a speech or a classroom lecture" (*Fulfilled in Your Hearing*, p. 24).

3. By avoiding fillers. Closely related to the misuse of language in the pulpit is the use of trite and hackneyed phrases that amount to fillers. "As I said before" is one of the most unnecessary and meaningless phrases. If it has already been said and has been said well, it needs no repetition. Another frequent phrase that has no meaning and in most instances is probably untrue is: "I could go on and on." Worst of all are the fillers that amount to an appeal for assent: "You know," "Don't get me wrong," the simple "Uh" grunt, and the oft-repeated "Okay?" which seems to imply that the congregation is either too young or too dull to follow, without prompting, the direction the homily is taking.

In the 1920s there was a fine third-grade teacher in Waverly, Iowa, who gave a memorable class in the art of speaking in public without using such expressions. Using the "grunt," she said, is an admission that the speaker doesn't know what to say next, and is filling an embarrassing moment of silence by employing this undistinguished single syllable. She then asked each student to recount for the class any interesting experiences that had happened during the past summer. She would ring a bell when the first grunt was uttered, mark the time, then go on to the next student. It was revealing that they could not talk for thirty seconds without using a filler. It was a remarkable and unforgettable lesson that not every moment of an address must be filled with sound. What a wise instructor, who taught this important lesson to young children, before their faulty speech habits could become ingrained. That lesson has still not been learned by many homilists who have had a thorough training in the art of public speaking. Try it yourself with a stopwatch when you practice the delivery of your next homily. Award yourself a star only when you have completed the entire homily without a grunt.

Technically, the grunt or filler is known as a vocalized hesitancy. The homilist who prides himself in not resorting to such fillers may be surprised to hear himself using them. As a matter of fact, vocalized hesitancies are highly contagious; if you hear another speaker uh-ing, or you-know-ing, the chances are you will catch the disability and do likewise.

4. *By staying on an adult level.* Another faulty use of language in the pulpit that decreases the credibility of the homilist is the employment of "kid" expressions when speaking to children, and especially when speaking to adults. Both groups dislike being talked down to. Children want to be grown up. Infants in the crib respond to baby language; those who have learned to tie their shoes do not. And adolescents, who have perfect antennas for the detection of anything fake, will immediately spot the grown-up who dons the mask of the teenager. Father Louis is a fine, deeply spiritual, and very committed priest. He works hard on his homilies. But unfortunately he uses the language of children at the weekend liturgy, and the parishioners have often complained that they feel as if they were sitting at little desks in a classroom instead of in pews.

5. *By appropriate gestures.* Almost every college course in public speaking will address the importance of using gestures. However, gestures should be used only if they come naturally to the speaker. The physical situation of the homilist, restricted by a stationary microphone and half-hidden by a pulpit or lectern, limits gesturing to movements of the head and a few hand motions in front of the chest area, unless of course he walks away from the pulpit. Perhaps the worst and most meaningless of all gestures is the one seen most frequently on commercials: the "chop," a distracting movement that causes the audience to follow the hands rather than the

thought. If gestures complement and make the words meaningful, they are a helpful addition to an address. If they are wooden and unnatural, they decrease the effect of the message. We have listened to powerful speakers who scarcely move a muscle during their presentation. Their messages are spellbinding because of their content and because the speakers have established their credibility. Mother Teresa is an example.

6. *Through eye contact.* We all suspect something untrustworthy about the person who will not look us in the eye. The technique of establishing visual contact with an entire congregation is a very simple one. As the speaker faces the audience, his eyes go to the back row and slowly go from right to left across that row, or vice versa; then he looks at those in the pews two or three rows toward the front, again going from left to right. When the process has been repeated several times, all in the audience will have the impression that their presence has been recognized. Having eye contact enables the audience to respond directly and immediately to the speaker. It also does the reverse: It enables the speaker to respond to the audience. A smile, a nodding of the head, a shaking of the head in disbelief, and a hundred other types of audience reaction provide invaluable feedback to the speaker and enable him to reinforce, repeat, or even modify the point being given.

We have already discussed in some detail two different methods of preparing and delivering a homily: using a manuscript and speaking from an outline. Credibility is not easy to promote when one reads a manuscript. Reading requires the eyes to be constantly fixed on the prepared text and restricts feedback from the audience. We speak here of reading a manuscript, not using one. Some of the finest speakers in our experience make use of a manuscript (not simply notes). Archbishop McNicholas, to whom we referred in the chapter on timing, would not go into the pulpit without a manuscript. His homilies were superb. He used the manuscript to prevent wandering and ad libbing. But before he preached he would commit the text to memory, so that the written document served only as a reminder of a particular word or phrase for which there was no adequate substitute. Some of the poorest homilies we have ever heard were given by preachers who prided themselves on never having a manuscript, on simply "getting on my feet and talking."

Father John, a much beloved priest who was known as a wanderer in the pulpit, described his homily as "treeing an idea and barking at it for a while." He was much admired for his personal qualities and for his learning, but not for his barking.

7. By *tone of voice*. Tone of voice will either contribute to or detract from the believability of a speaker. If an elevated or a lower tone is not natural to a speaker, it should not be used. Bishop Tim had a tenor voice. For some reason he admired the bass and baritone quality of some of his favorite speakers and tried his best to emulate them in the pulpit. For those who knew him, the result was humorous; inevitably there was a loss of credibility.

8. By *facial expression*. The homilist can win credibility by reflecting the mood of the occasion. He should normally walk into the pulpit smiling. The Liturgy of the Word is an occasion for rejoicing; the Good News is about to be preached. Audiences react positively to a smile. It makes them realize that the preacher enjoys his work. If the homilist is not happy and enthusiastic in the pulpit, one might ask, "Why not?" Why should not a priest or deacon be excited about the most joyful message ever heard? Why should he not be enthusiastic about the most important part of his week, the moment he is able to share that Good News with the congregation? Why should not one who is given the privilege of offering the Body and Blood of Christ be uplifted and cheerful during those grace-filled moments? The audience responds quickly to the dourness or the cheerfulness, the joy or the dejection of the speaker. We have always been puzzled by the priest or minister who is smiling, relaxed, and friendly when greeting the parishioners before the service, will adopt the same mien at the church door when asking the departing congregation about their families, but will appear unhappy during the service itself. It would be more understandable if the situation were reversed. When the preacher enters the pulpit smiling he is saying to the congregation: "What a joyful experience; we are about to hear the Word of God." Imagine the reaction of the congregation to a preacher who declares—with sad countenance and in a sepulchral tone—that he is about to proclaim the Good News of salvation to the people.

9. By *posture*. A relaxed posture and delivery is an aid to believability. Some homilists walk back and forth in front of the con-

gregation during the homily. If that is natural and comfortable for the speaker, well and good. If it is not consistent with his personality and usual form of delivery, it will be seen as acting. We do not think it a good communication technique to walk up and down the aisle, causing the homilist to have his back to a portion of the congregation.

10. By asking the possible. Care should be taken not to ask for the impossible. The homilist is doing that when he preaches on reverence for the Eucharist, and tells his congregation that proper respect for the sacrament will mean that no one will ever leave the church until after the final blessing. Monsignor Bob Ferring tells about the time he was carrying on a campaign to have everyone stay until the Mass was completed. He stationed himself outside the front door of the church one Sunday. When a young woman came running down the steps before the liturgy was concluded, he asked her, "*Must* you leave Mass early?" Without breaking stride, she answered, "Yes."

11. By sharing himself. Finally, the homilist attains credibility through sharing himself. The congregation is interested in knowing who the homilist is. He should not be afraid to tell stories about his childhood, adolescence, and early ministry. Sharing examples of how prayer in his home, lenten practices of his family, and instructions from his parents led him to place a high value on spirituality and on being a priest will help develop and strengthen the faith of parishioners. "Who do people say that I am," asked Christ, knowing that the topic had been frequently discussed among his disciples. The congregation wants to know the individual who is asking them to follow Christ. They want to know how he reacts to life's situations. "I get discouraged when . . . I get nervous if I am. . . . I am the worst auto mechanic in the world. I am a very poor putter. I enjoy Mozart, or Glenn Miller, John Denver, the Beatles, and I am a Cubs fan." The congregation can identify with the speaker who says in so many words, "I am just like everyone else in this church. I make mistakes. I have faults. I like chocolate, and I dislike liver. Sometimes I am proud and distant. I am not very good at mathematics. I am not the best homilist in the world, but I keep trying. Yesterday I missed a three-foot putt. I double faulted on match point in my tennis game. I am just trying to get to heaven, like you. I sometimes wonder if I am good enough to make it."

The congregation wants to know what kind of family the homilist comes from. "I loved and respected my dad. I still remember that the greatest kindness my mom ever showed my dad was to laugh at his jokes, even when she had heard them a hundred times. I fought with my sisters and got very angry when they borrowed my shirts, but since we've grown up we've became fond of one another, and one of my greatest joys is to visit their homes." Ed Macauley opens many of his talks and homilies by relating personal experiences from his basketball, broadcasting, and business careers. These revelations unveil the homilist before his congregation. They see him as one of them, sharing their struggles to love and serve God, aware of their weaknesses because he, too, must work each day to come closer to the Lord.

The sharing of personal experiences is one of the keys to success of Marriage Encounter. The couples and priests on the weekend do not teach principles for successful living in marriage. They simply relate the struggles and pains they have experienced in working out a relationship with their spouse (the spouse of the priest on the weekend is the people whom he serves in his present capacity), and talk about how they have solved difficult problems that came into their lives, and what the result has been in their marriage and in their priesthood.

The homilist's personal sharings should be those that are similar to experiences the congregation has had, and are related to the message of the readings. The audience becomes involved. Their reaction is usually, "That's just like the time I . . ." or "He is human, just as I am."

EM: I often share with congregations the story of our son Patrick, who contracted spinal meningitis in Boston during my final year with the Boston Celtics. The disease completely destroyed his brain and he was a cerebral palsy child. He never walked or talked and never recognized his parents, brothers, or sisters. He died when he was thirteen. The day he died, I was driving my car and there were tears in my eyes because Patrick was gone. But suddenly I realized that Patrick was just fine. I could almost hear him say, "Dad, don't worry about me." I realized he had lived a perfect life, far better than my own.

FF: Many of my sharings with congregations involve my family. I tell them stories about my parents, my brothers and sisters, and my grandparents. These stories tell the congregation who we are. And who we are shapes the messages they receive from us.

There is one caution. Every successful technique in preaching can be misused and overused. The sharing of feelings with the congregation should not become a daily practice. One is reminded of the television reporter whose first and only question for people involved in deep tragedy is: "How do you feel about losing your home?" A congregation can weary of listening too often to the personal reflections of a homilist. We have heard many complaints about priests or deacons who begin *every* homily with a story about their growing up.

It is often said that the Christian faith is not a faith in doctrinal matters, but a commitment to a person, Jesus Christ. In some ways it is also the person of the homilist that is the principal determinant for which of the pulpit utterances the congregation will accept and believe. It is true that the message itself, the Gospel, is the Good News, and nothing can take its place. But the degree to which the astonishing truth of the Paschal Mystery becomes a part of the audience is very much dependent on the messenger. If he is not an actor on a stage, if he is genuine, projects authenticity, and is believable, many roadblocks to the acceptance and conviction of the congregation have been removed.

— 13 —

The Judge Does Not
Always Give Tens

You must expect occasional disagreement and failure

Two fears prevent individuals from improving: fear of disagreement and the fear of failure. Yet for anyone who speaks, writes, or performs in the public eye, whether he is a homilist, politician, writer, athlete, or teacher, disagreement and failure are inevitable, and not entirely negative consequences of entering the public forum.

Disagreement and failure are inescapable for the homilist for the simple reason that his responsibility is to preach Jesus Christ. In spite of Christ's resurrection, the Pentecostal gift of tongues of fire, and the witness of generations of heroic Christians who shed their blood in testimony of their faith, the teachings of Christ have not been received with universal agreement these past two thousand years. Many people the world over reject his message, and many who claim Christianity as their heritage, and some members of every congregation, accept it selectively. Hilaire Belloc once said that Christianity has not failed; it has never been tried.

Preaching the Word of God means addressing controversial topics. It means asserting what God says about helping the poor, about drugs, spousal abuse, abortion, spending one's time in prayer, and forgiving those who have offended us. It means discussing even the unpleasant elements of our faith: final judgment, purgatory, and hell. These topics make us aware that it is wrong to be greedy, selfish, and unforgiving; they remind us that we need to prepare for the future life. Not all of these messages are easy to accept. Sometimes the better the communicator, the more disagreement he will evoke and the more failures he will experience, precisely because he is explicit and unequivocal in his call for listeners to adopt a different lifestyle. Jesus elicited no disagreement from his disciples when his statements about the Eucharist were subtle and indirect. But when he definitively taught his disciples that doctrine in the synagogue at Capernaum, they murmured, "'This saying is hard; who can accept it?' [Afterward] many of his disciples returned to their former way of life and no longer accompanied him" (John 6:59–66). Disagreement and failure are closely related outcomes of a homily; yet they differ in some ways, and we shall discuss them separately.

Fear of Disagreement

Can you imagine the result if, at the end of your homily, five randomly selected members of the congregation would stand up and flash rating cards? Would all of them give tens in judging your homily? Would *any* of them give tens? Would you be willing to face this sort of evaluation? We do not recommend it, but wish to make the point that some congregation members will reject your message; some will deplore your delivery. How do you face these judges?

Of course, the homilist can avoid disagreement if he preaches bland homilies, not asking the congregation for any action or commitment. He may discuss the beautiful life that God has in store for us without making any suggestion that life with God requires more than the typical response often asked by the TV evangelist: "Stand up, walk up to the pulpit and declare that you accept Jesus as your savior."

Disagreement is also avoided when the homilist chooses as the invariable goal of the homily either education or praise. No one will resist an educational homily, if it is skillfully prepared and presented. Praise usually evokes universal approval. But a steady diet of homilies using only these goals soon becomes banal, boring, and tiresome. When you alter your goal and try to motivate the listeners, inspire them, chastise them, encourage them to improve their spiritual lives, or to take specific action, you can expect disagreement. The reaction is likely to be, "Leave me alone. Why are you trying to interfere with my life?"

The results of disagreement can be divisive for the parish and painful to the homilist. However, there *are* ways the homilist can deliver even challenging messages without eliciting serious and permanent disagreement from the assembly. One is to vary the goal and objective of the homily. Changing goal and objective has a positive effect on a congregation. If you ask the parishioners to make some hard decisions on a particular Sunday, you can follow on the next Sunday with a homily that praises them for their accomplishments. Variation in the goal and objective of the homily will assure them that the speaker is not basically negative.

Another way of blunting disagreement while preaching tough homilies is to seek feedback from the congregation. You can do this by preparing the homily with a representative group of parishioners who will be asked to suggest relevant and specific local problems to address, as well as methods of approaching those problems that will not antagonize and alienate the congregation. A second, more radical, and more delicate method of obtaining feedback, used by very few speakers, is to encourage actual discussion of an issue by the congregation immediately after Mass. The process is touchy, and requires a great deal of acceptance and genuine listening on the part of the homilist, but if done with obvious concern for the parishioners and respect for differing opinions, it can be effective. The value of either method is that the congregation has input into the content of the Sunday homily, either directly or through its representatives, and is not a silent partner in the Liturgy of the Word.

While the homilist should use every technique that will reduce unnecessary disagreement to a minimum, controversy cannot be totally avoided if he is to be a good preacher. Popularity is one thing; effectiveness is another. The treatment of serious matters from the pulpit involving moral issues that are politically divisive will *always* elicit some objections. Conflict goes with the territory. The homilist who experiences negative reactions to his homily from time to time should realize that he is in good company. Even after performing miracles of healing, restoring people to life, and feeding the multitude, Christ had many detractors. Eventually they crucified him.

When we say that the homilist should not shy away from "hard" topics, we are *not* suggesting that every topic has a legitimate place in the pulpit. One example is politics. The homily is not the proper forum for strictly political issues, and most dioceses have published policies defining the approach the homilist should take toward such matters. The church's role is to call attention to the moral and religious dimensions of issues. It has an obligation to present Gospel values as norms for social and political life, and to indicate the demands of the Christian faith for the transformation of society. However, the church and its leaders must affirm, not threaten, the political process and genuine pluralism. Several dioceses have published guidelines for political involvement of diocesan officials, clergy, religious, parish councils and parish organizations.

Fear of Failure

The second fear facing the homilist is that of failure. While disagreement is likely to be perceived by the homilist as a personal rejection, failure is often perceived as a personal inadequacy. A sense of failure comes when the homilist sees members of the congregation yawning or fidgeting or even sleeping during the homily. Failure is perceived when a congregation fails to carry out suggestions for action presented in the homily. Failure is experienced when members of the congregation go beyond simple disagreement and actively oppose the recommendations or teachings of the homilist.

Christ, too, experienced failure. However, there is more to the story than saying that Christ failed in many ways, and therefore the homilist should not fear personal defeats. What happened to Christ is part of a mystery that points to a design for Christian living. St. Paul teaches that mystery, and although he did not use the term himself, today's theologians have labeled it the Paschal Mystery of Christ.

Stated in the simplest possible terms, the Paschal Mystery means that every Christian must in some way pass through the same kind of suffering, disillusionment, and pain that Christ experienced if he expects to share in Christ's resurrection. The principal part of the mystery is a fact that sheds light on many of life's puzzles. It is God's plan that every success, every glorious moment, every great achievement must be preceded by some kind of dying, some form of suffering, some type of disillusionment. The lesson to be learned in the Paschal Mystery is that failure was not present in the life of Christ by accident, but as part of God's plan. If we are Christ's disciples, failure needs to be a part of our plan. To understand this takes some of the pain out of failure, and adds another dimension to suffering. Every farmer has an intuitive understanding of the Paschal Mystery. "Unless the grain of wheat falls into the ground and dies, it cannot produce fruit." For the homilist, it is helpful to know that failure in his communication is not a disaster.

There is probably no occupation that better exemplifies the principle that past failures increase the probability of future success than athletics. Athletes know the meaning of "no pain, no gain."

EM: Please don't think me egotistical when I list my accomplishments in the world of basketball. I need to state these facts to make a point. I was an all-state player in high school. In college I was a two-time All American. When I played with the Boston Celtics I was an All NBA player three times. I was the Most Valuable Player in the first NBA All Star game. I was the youngest player ever inducted into the Basketball Hall of Fame. I was a superstar, I guess. All of which, plus fifty cents, will get me a cup of coffee, but not much more.

Now let's examine my entry into the game of basketball. As an eighth grader I played on a team that did not win a game. We were 0-13. One game we were shut out, 33-0. That doesn't happen often in basketball. I was awkward, tall, and weak, and not very aggressive. As a high school freshman I did not play basketball. I had a typing class after school. That class helped me write this book but it didn't help my progress in the world of athletics. As a sophomore I was on the B team as the substitute center. As a freshman in college, I guarded All American seven-foot Bob Kurland the night he scored fifty-eight points, an NCAA record. My first three months as a pro with the St. Louis Bombers, I was anything but out-standing.

So, how did I ever become a good player? It was very simple. I failed, and failed, and failed some more. But every time I failed I said "What did I do wrong?" I then practiced alone to correct the fault and went out and tried again. So I established a pattern: I failed, I made corrections, I practiced, and I tried again. I kept repeating the process. Never did I say, "I failed, so I won't continue trying to improve." Genuine failure is not learning from unsuccessful efforts.

What happened? Others stopped trying. I kept practicing. Where I failed six months ago, I was now better. I practiced the jump shot for hundreds of hours. In high school I was a good shooter. In my first college game I turned to shoot a jump shot and the defensive man slapped it right back in my face. What did I learn? First, I had to develop another shot. I began to practice a hook shot, right- and left-handed. I scored hundreds of points with the hook shot. No one, except Bill Russell, ever blocked that shot. But he blocked everyone's shots, so I didn't feel bad. Second, I realized that if I could fake the jump shot and get the defensive man up in the air, I could drive past him for easy shots. I scored thousands of points with that move. Third, I still had the jump shot, and with the other two options available, the defense would be less inclined to leave their feet to block it. When I started, I had a jump shot. When it failed, I didn't quit. After hours of practice, I had three different options, and the defensive man was in trouble. I learned from my failures.

I spent ten years in the NBA. How does one become a professional basketball player? By experimenting with different techniques, then saving the ones that succeed and discarding those that fail. Actually, it could have been devastating to my ego to fail but I understood the value of failure. As I played against Bob Pettit, George Mikan, Bill Russell, Bob Cousy, and other Hall of Famers I knew that I would not outscore them every night. But I learned something from each encounter and I improved my own techniques. When playing against the greatest competition in the world, I knew there would be times when I would have my brains beaten out. I knew too, that if I had the right attitude in facing failure, I would succeed. That is why I'm particularly proud of the fact that my greatest scoring night in the NBA was forty-six points against George Mikan and the Minneapolis Lakers, the perennial NBA champs during the early 1950s.

When I was learning, I expected failure, because I continued to seek out and find better players to play against. I lost, but I learned. As others lost, they stopped. I kept trying and pretty soon there weren't many players better than I.

Some people say I am a good speaker. How did I become a good speaker? By using the same philosophy. I was willing to fail as I developed my techniques. Not only was I willing to fail, I expected to fail. When I told a joke, when I tried to be emotional, when I tried to pace my voice, when I tried to use gestures, when I tried to tell people what I thought they should do to become better, I was always happy when I succeeded. I was also happy when I failed. Why? Because after I failed I could study my technique and figure out what I had done wrong. So, after two tries, or six, or twenty, I would succeed. Then I didn't have to worry about that mistake any more and could go on to correct another one.

I still fail, but that never discouraged me in the past, and it doesn't now. It is very humbling to stand before an audience and to know that "you have lost them." But instead of having my ego demolished, I try to convert the experience to a positive situation. I ask myself "Why did I lose them?" As I answer that question, I am ready to face another audience and then I usually do a better job. Not perfect, but better.

I believe that one of the surest routes to improvement is to look upon failure as a great learning opportunity. To seize the opportunity, study it, learn from it, and say, "Now let's try it again, and again, and maybe again." When speaking, we often think it would be a catastrophe if we make a mistake. Yet ninety percent of the time when I make a mistake in speaking, the audience does not even know it. I know what I am trying to do; they don't. So when I fail, it's not really a humiliating experience.

When I try something new in preaching, if it succeeds, wonderful! If it does not, the audience doesn't get angry; they don't disagree with me, they just don't listen. If I am not successful I am disappointed. It hurts a bit. But it is a learning experience, and I will analyze what went wrong, and will be back again, and again, and again, until I get it right.

And, so, failure and disagreement, if handled properly, can serve as aids rather than hindrances to successful communication. We have seen speakers go through the agony of experimentation, and have seen them fail. They are disappointed for a few moments, but success is all the sweeter when it eventually comes. We have also seen homilists who never try to improve, who never take a chance, who never experiment, who never say "Maybe I could be better." These speakers continue on a mediocre track and their disappointment mounts year after year.

Trying to improve can guarantee failure, but it also guarantees success. Instead of fearing failure and worrying about whether a congregation will disagree, the homilist should accept the fact that those conditions are the price anyone pays for success and ultimate satisfaction.

Part Four

What the Fundamentals Produce

— 14 —

If You Build It . . .

Putting it all together

In the movie *Field of Dreams* the main character of the story hears a voice telling him that if he builds a baseball diamond in his corn-field in Iowa, famous baseball players from the distant past, now deceased, would come to play on it, especially Shoeless Joe Jackson. "If you build it, he will come." He builds it—over everyone's objections—and Jackson and the others come.

Field of Dreams, a low budget picture, surprised everyone by becoming a great hit. A basic truth was conveyed in it: If someone has faith and perseverance and works hard, success will follow. We are confident that a homilist who works with faith and perseverance to improve his homilies, building on the fundamentals of good homiletic communication, will improve very much. But here is a suggestion concerning the study and application of those fundamentals.

The reader who agrees with the importance of the fundamentals might try all ten when preparing his next homily. That would be a mistake. You should adopt the technique used by most successful athletes: Tackle one problem at a time, perfect that fundamental, then move on to the next one. To give an example, a basketball player needs to work on a number of objectives as he masters the jump shot. Each part of the body must function properly. The eyes should stay on the rim of the basket; the elbow is under the back of the hand at the top of the shot and not outside that plane; the wrist must be cocked; the follow-through should go directly toward the basket; the legs, feet, fingers, and other parts of the body need to be in the proper position.

Learning the fundamentals one at a time requires intelligent practice, self-evaluation, and, if available, outside advice. Success doesn't come overnight. The great players are willing to spend the hours needed practicing on the playground, in the gym, during the off season. He or she doesn't have time to master the fundamentals while learning the plays, the offense, the defense, and preparing for games. And so, constant practice is required, but it must be intelligent practice. If the proper fundamentals are not pursued, the athlete will be practicing mistakes.

We have outlined a series of fundamentals of communication that will, when used properly, assist anyone who wishes to improve homilies. Don't make the mistake of trying to use all ten fundamentals in your next homily.

EM: I played competitive basketball for nineteen years. After that, I continued to coach and teach for the next thirty-four years. I am still teaching the fundamentals of the game.

Some people look on the practice of fundamentals as hard work but I don't. I enjoyed the solitary hours on the court, perfecting the position of elbow, eyes, and wrist. I enjoyed playing against better players when I was young, fully realizing that I would be beaten. That was not a problem. I wanted to face better competition so that I could recognize which areas of my game were deficient. Then I would go back and practice those techniques until I had mastered them. It is a great thrill to lose to someone by a lopsided score and then slowly improve and eventually beat that competitor. It happened to me only because I was willing to spend the necessary time to improve, while others were not.

Don't be overwhelmed by the size of the task facing you in trying to master a large group of fundamentals. Look at parts of the picture and ask, "Can I reach this individual objective?" Yes you can if you are willing to spend the time. Success in basketball comes when someone hands you a medal and says, "You are one of the best." Success comes to the homilist when one of the congregation comes to you and says, "That was a fine homily; you have taught me something"; or when someone pays you the highest compliment a homilist can receive: a simple "Thank you for your homily."

Our suggestion is this: Study the ten fundamentals outlined in this book. Then pick one and, as you prepare your next homily, consciously try to apply that fundamental. Suppose you select *interest* as the first fundamental you wish to work on. Scan the local newspaper during the week to find what might be of special interest to your congregation. Then study the Sunday readings and discover what messages are contained in them. Next, determine how the interest factor underlying those messages is related to reports in the newspaper and to the interests of your congregation. The news may have included accounts of prejudice, bigotry, the rising crime rate, local or national politics, unemployment, stories of bravery in fires or accidents, parent-teen relationships, and others. Take one of those stories and use it in your homily.

If you choose to begin with the fundamental *specific*, you might close your homily with words such as, "This is the message found in Scripture today, and this is what you and I can do about it." Then give a specific course of action. The action could be as simple as praying, or asking your congregation to attend a school board meeting, or to study the platform of current candidates for office.

During the month, stay with that one fundamental. As you make use of it week after week, you will find it easier to incorporate it into your homily. Emulate the successful athlete who works on a single fundamental until that process becomes automatic.

EM: I worked on the individual fundamentals of basketball until my body reacted automatically when called upon to execute each action. In sports, that is called "muscle memory." Muscles learn to react spontaneously so that you don't have to clutter up your mind with a hundred thoughts. Muscle memory comes only after repeating a particular movement thousands of times.

When the month ends, ask some individuals in the congregation, "Have you noticed anything in particular about my recent homilies?" Often you'll find that they will comment on the fundamental you have been working on in your presentations.

After the month is over, pick a second fundamental and work on it while still using the first one. Suppose the fundamental is identifying a *goal*. Select a goal for your homily, but on the next four Sundays vary that goal, using a different one for each homily. In succeeding months, go through the same process with the remaining fundamentals. Above all, don't be discouraged.

> EM: I did not get my first award in basketball until I had been playing the game for five years. When I made All American I had been playing for nine years, and I didn't make the All Pro team until I had played eleven years.

Ten months of your time (one for each fundamental) is a small investment to make in order to gain the personal satisfaction of knowing you are becoming a more effective homilist. During the ten-month period, tape each of your homilies, then listen to the tape before you start preparing for next Sunday's homily. Examine whether or not you really did use the fundamental you were working on. Will congregations react negatively to the taping of your homily? Just the opposite. Most homilists of our acquaintance who tape their homilies find their congregation delighted that they are making efforts to improve their presentations.

We suggest, too, that during those ten months you have at least four of your homilies videotaped. Review them carefully. After the sixth month, check your progress. A very effective way to do this is to take a written survey of your parishioners, and ask them, "How are my homilies?" It will not be ego-lifting, but it is sure to be a rewarding experience. A survey is the easiest way to determine what steps you need to take to improve your homilies. Athletic teams spend millions of dollars filming their games so they can see their mistakes and correct them. You have a ready-made, inexpensive source of counsel in the members of your congregation. Don't be afraid to ask them; they will be happy you asked and pleased to help.

A sample survey will be found at the end of this chapter. It includes questions involving the use of the ten fundamentals. Give it to your parishioners. If the questionnaire does not touch on all the areas you would like to explore, make up one of your own. When the results are in, determine which of the evaluations are legitimate (usually the ones repeated most often). Even if you disagree with their comments, pay close attention to each criticism. Don't become defensive and think, "They don't know what they are talking about."

EM: I once suggested to a priest that he have his congregation complete a homily survey. He said he would never do such a thing. When I asked why, he replied, "Because most of the people in my congregation wouldn't know how to evaluate a good homily." In other words, "Even if my congregation doesn't believe my homilies are of any value to them, I'll be the sole judge of how good those homilies are."

Try to incorporate their suggestions into your future homilies—again, one at a time. Asking for comments from your parishioners is a challenging experience. Some homilists will never do it. It is, however, one of the most enlightening exercises you can carry out. And, who knows? Some in your congregation may even say, "We can tell that you place a high value on homilies because you are working on them so hard. Thank you for spending so much of your time and talent on messages that have so much meaning in our lives."

Homily Survey

The purpose of this survey is to determine your reaction to the homilies you have heard during the last six months. It is not necessary to sign the survey, but it would be helpful to us to have the following information about yourself:

Sex ____   Age____   Marital Status ____

Read the statements below, and circle the number that comes closest to your reactions to the homilies you have heard.

STATEMENT	STRONGLY AGREE	AGREE	DISAGREE	STRONGLY DISAGREE
The homilies I hear:				
Are applicable to my daily life	1	2	3	4
Have a variety of messages such as motivation, inspiration, praise, criticism, education	1	2	3	4
Have a single topic	1	2	3	4
Are addressed to all age groups in the congregation	1	2	3	4
Address specific situations	1	2	3	4
Ask for specific action or a change in attitude	1	2	3	4
Are well prepared and organized	1	2	3	4
Are spoken in plain language by a homilist who appears to be genuine and believable	1	2	3	4

STATEMENT	STRONGLY AGREE	AGREE	DISAGREE	STRONGLY DISAGREE
Can be easily heard and followed	1	2	3	4
Touch on difficult topics from time to time in a straightforward way (such as charity, youth, prayer, drugs, sex)	1	2	3	4
Are too long (circle 1) too short (circle 2) just right (circle 3)	1	2	3	

The homilies I hear are (circle one)	Excellent	Good	Fair	Poor

If the homilies you hear are "good" or "excellent," state why you have that opinion.

If they are "poor" or "fair," why?

If you are not satisfied with the homilies you hear, what should the homilist do to improve?

If you are not satisfied with the homilies, what should the (arch)diocese, deanery, synod, etc., do to help the homilist improve them?

What sort of things should you hear, or in what way should a homily be delivered for you to consider it a good homily?

Bibliography

We include the publications cited in the text and a few others we believe readers would find helpful. The bibliography is intentionally brief. We did not find many books that connect substantially with our approach to homiletics, and we judged that readers would be interested in hearing what we have to say about homilies, rather than offer a synopsis of what is already available. In keeping with our belief that homiletics services should be used only after the main preparation of a homily has been completed, we have included only two.

Works Cited in *Homilies Alive*

Brown, Raymond E., et al. *Jerome Biblical Commentary*. Prentice Hall, 1968.

Cormier, Jay. *Giving Good Homilies*. Ave Maria Press, 1984. A brief but clear discussion of homiletics as a communication skill.

Fant, Clyde E. *Preaching for Today*. Harper & Row, 1975. An attempt to unify the practice of preaching by integrating the theory of proclamation with sermon construction and delivery.

McNulty, Frank J. (ed). *Preaching Better*. Paulist Press, 1985. A practical work, bringing together the thoughts of communication specialists. Fresh approaches on storytelling and on the use of the imagination in preaching.

U.S. Catholic Conference, *Fulfilled in Your Hearing: The Homily in the Sunday Assembly*. 1982. A practical booklet published by the Bishops' Committee on Priestly Life in Ministry.

Recommended Books

Anonymous. *Love in the Gospels, by a Modern Pilgrim*. Thomas More Press, 1982. Thirty-seven brief but sparkling chapters viewing the Good News as a source book on love, human and divine.

Barclay, William. *The Daily Study Bible Series*. Westminster Press, 1975. A scholarly commentary designed for devotional reading and Bible study. A wealth of details.

Bausch, William J. *Storytelling: Imagination and Faith*. Twenty-Third Publications, 1984. Rediscovering the art of storytelling as a means of arriving at spiritual truths. Incorporates philosophical insights into the process of weaving a homily around famous stories from different cultures. For examples of Bausch's style, see his volumes of homilies: *Timely Homilies; Telling Stories, Compelling Stories;* and *More Telling Stories, Compelling Stories* (all from Twenty-Third Publications).

Burghardt, Walter J., S.J. *Preaching, The Art and the Craft.* Paulist Press, 1987. By the acknowledged dean of preaching in America. He emphasizes a return to the Bible for inspiration and content, a deepening awareness of the link between liturgy, Scripture, and the homily, and the importance of imagination in preaching.

Edwards, O.C. *The Living and Active Word.* Seabury Press, 1975. Shows how the words of Heb. 4:12 ("The word of God is living and active, sharper than any two-edged sword") can be made effective through carrying out four steps in homily preparation. Selected sermons exemplify the method.

Finley, James F., C.S.P. *Wake Up and Preach.* Alba House, 1986. Thirteen commandments for reaching today's congregations, with their different levels of age, background, and education.

Milhaven, Annie Lally (ed). *Sermons Seldom Heard.* Crossroad, 1991. Contributions from female preachers covering topics of women's experience.

Maly, Eugene H. *The Word Alive.* Alba House, 1982. Reflections and commentaries on the Sunday readings.

Marcheschi, Graziano and Nancy Seitz Marcheschi. *Workbook for Lectors and Gospel Readers.* Archdiocese of Chicago, Liturgy Training Publications, 1990. An annual publication based on the current liturgical cycle. Offers excellent interpretations and suggestions for the Sunday readings and for reading Scripture aloud. Useful for both lectors and homilists.

McNulty, Frank J. (ed.) *Preaching Better.* Paulist Press, 1985. Good advice from experienced preachers.

Muehl, William. *Why Preach? Why Listen?* Fortress Press, 1986. Seeks to relate lay experience to theological categories and to examine the lay side of the dialogue between pulpit and pew.

Stuhlmueller, Carroll, C.P. *Biblical Meditations.* Paulist Press, 1980. Five volumes. A combination of scriptural reflection and prayer experience for the liturgical seasons.

Young, Robert D. *Be Brief About It: Clues to Effective Preaching.* Westminster Press, 1980. An enlargement on the suggestions made in Chapter 10 of *Homilies Alive.* Brevity has a profound influence on both speaker and listener. Ten guidelines for preparing brief homilies, with examples.

Homiletic Services

Homily Helps. Cincinnati, St. Anthony Messenger. Exegesis, summary of the message, attention-getters with application, and transition to Liturgy of the Eucharist.

Celebration. Box 419493, Kansas City, MO 64141. Weekly Commentary on the Scripture, planning suggestions, possible themes, and sample homily. Helpful for homilists and liturgists.